YEAR A
AFTER PENTECOST 2

YEAR A
AFTER PENTECOST 2

PREACHING
THE REVISED
COMMON
LECTIONARY

Marion Soards
Thomas Dozeman
Kendall McCabe

ABINGDON PRESS
Nashville

PREACHING THE REVISED COMMON LECTIONARY
YEAR A: AFTER PENTECOST 2

This book is printed on recycled, acid-free paper.

Library of Congress Cataloging-in-Publication Data
(Revised for vol. 4)

Soards, Marion L., 1952–
    Preaching the revised Common lectionary.
    Includes index.
    Contents: [1] Advent/Christmas/Epiphany—
[4] After Pentecost 2.
    1. Bible—Liturgical lessons, English. 2. Bible—
Homiletical use. I. Dozeman, Thomas B. II. McCabe,
Kendall, 1939–   . III. Common lectionary.
BS391.2.S59   1992   251   91-34039
    ISBN 0-687-33800-X (v. 1: alk. paper)
    ISBN 0-687-33801-8 (v. 2: alk. paper)
    ISBN 0-687-33872-7 (v. 3: alk. paper)
    ISBN 0-687-33871-9 (v. 4: alk. paper)

93 94 95 96 97 98 99 00 01 02 — 10 9 8 7 6 5 4 3 2

MANUFACTURED IN THE UNITED STATES OF AMERICA

Contents

CONTENTS

Introduction

Now pastors and students have a systematic treatment of essential issues of the Christian year and Bible study for worship and proclamation based on the Revised Common Lectionary. Interpretation of the lectionary will separate into three parts: Calendar, Canon, and Celebration. A brief word of introduction will provide helpful guidelines for utilizing this resource in worship through the Christian year.

Calendar. Every season of the Christian year will be introduced with a theological interpretation of its meaning, and how it relates to the overall Christian year. This section will also include specific liturgical suggestions for the season.

Canon. The lectionary passages will be interpreted in terms of their setting, structure, and significance. First, the word *setting* is being used loosely in this commentary to include a range of different contexts in which biblical texts can be interpreted from literary setting to historical or cultic settings. Second, regardless of how the text is approached under the heading of setting, interpretation will always proceed to an analysis of the structure of the text under study. Third, under the heading of significance, central themes and motifs of the passage will be underscored to provide a theological interpretation of the text as a springboard for preaching. Thus interpretation of the lectionary passages will result in the outline on the next page.

Celebration. This section will focus on specific ways of relating the lessons to liturgical acts and/or homiletical options for the day on which they occur. How the texts have been used in the Christian tradition will sometimes be illustrated to stimulate the thinking of preachers and planners of worship services.

I. OLD TESTAMENT TEXTS

A. The Old Testament Lesson

1. Setting

2. Structure

3. Significance

B. Psalm

1. Setting

2. Structure

3. Significance

II. NEW TESTAMENT TEXTS

A. The Epistle

1. Setting

2. Structure

3. Significance

B. The Gospel

1. Setting

2. Structure

3. Significance

Why We Use the Lectionary

Although many denominations have been officially or unofficially using some form of the lectionary for many years some pastors are still unclear about where it comes from, why some lectionaries differ from denomination to denomination, and why the use of a lectionary is to be preferred to a more random sampling of scripture.

Simply put, the use of a lectionary provides a more diverse scriptural diet for God's people, and it can help protect the congregation from the whims and prejudices of the pastor and other worship planners. Faithful use of the lectionary means that preachers must deal with texts they would rather ignore, but about which the congregation may have great concern and interest. The stories of Israel's experience in the wilderness, or Paul's understanding of the return of Christ, which we encounter in this volume, might be cases in point. Adherence to the lectionary can be an antidote to that homiletical arrogance which says, "I know what my people need," and in humility acknowledges that the Word of God found in scripture may speak to more needs on Sunday morning than we even know exist, when we seek to proclaim faithfully the message we have wrestled from the text.

The lectionary may also serve as a resource for liturgical content. The psalm is intended to be a response to the Old Testament lesson, and not read as a lesson itself, but beyond that the lessons may inform the content of prayers of confession, intercession, and petition. Some lessons may be adapted as affirmations of faith, as in *The United Methodist Hymnal,* nos. 887-889; the United Church of Christ's *Hymnal,* nos. 429-430; and the Presbyterian *Worshipbook,* no. 30. The "Celebration" entries for each day will call attention to these opportunities from time to time.

Pastors and preachers in the free-church tradition should think of the lectionary as a primary resource for preaching and worship, but need to remember that the lectionary was made for them and not they for the lectionary. The lectionary may serve as the inspiration for a separate series of lessons and sermons that will include texts not in the present edition, or having chosen one of the lectionary passages as the basis for the day's sermon, the preacher may wish to make an independent choice of the other lessons to supplement and illustrate the primary text. The lectionary will be of most value when its use is not a cause for legalism but for inspiration.

Just as there are no perfect preachers, there are no perfect lectionaries. The Revised Common Lectionary, upon which this series is based, is the result of the work of many years by the Consultation on Common Texts and is a response to ongoing evaluation of the *Common Lectionary* (1983) by pastors and scholars from the several participating denominations. The current interest in the lectionary can be traced back to the Second Vatican Council, which ordered lectionary revision for the Roman Catholic Church:

> The treasures of the Bible are to be opened up more lavishly, so that richer fare may be provided for the faithful at the table of God's Word. In this way a more representative portion of the holy Scriptures will be read to the people over a set cycle of years. (*The Documents of Vatican II*, Walter Abbott, ed. [Piscataway, N.J.: New Century, 1974], p. 155)

The example thus set by Roman Catholics inspired Protestants to take more seriously the place of the Bible in their services and sermons, and soon many denominations had issued their own three-year cycles, based generally on the Roman Catholic model but with their own modifications. This explains why some discrepancies and variations appear in different forms of the lectionary. The Revised Common Lectionary (RCL) is an effort to increase agreement among the churches. A table at the end of the volume will list the differences between the RCL and the Roman Catholic, Episcopal, and Lutheran lectionaries. Where no entry is made, all are in agreement with the RCL.

For those unacquainted with the general pattern of the lectionary, a brief word of explanation may be helpful for sermon preparation. (1) The three years are each distinguished by one of the Synoptic Gospels: Matthew in A, Mark in B, Luke in C. John is distributed over the three years with a heavy emphasis during Lent and Easter. (2) Two types of readings are used. During the periods of Advent to Epiphany and Lent to Pentecost, the readings are usually topical, that is, there is some common theme among them. During the Sundays after Epiphany and Pentecost the readings are continuous, with no necessary connection between the lessons. In the period covered by this volume, we continue to hear of the experience of the children of Israel in the desert, their crossing into the Promised Land, and their experience under the Judges. The Old Testament readings are from the Pentateuch in recognition of Matthew's concern to portray the church as the continuation of the sacred history which begins with God's promise to Abraham. The epistle lessons place us in the New Testament churches at Philippi and Thessalonica, and we are invited to share in the lives of those congregations as they struggle with the meaning of the Easter proclamation for them and wait for the appearing of the Lord. These are bold, general themes, and are intended to provide a theological environment for homiletical thought rather than a thematic outline between all three lessons from week to week. Perhaps it should also be added that though the psalm is intended to be a response by the people to the Old Testament lesson—rather than as a lesson on its own—this in no way suggests that it cannot be used as the text for the sermon.

This is the fourth of four volumes that deal with the lessons for the entire A Cycle of the Christian year. Volume 1 covers Advent through the time after Epiphany. Volume 2 includes Ash Wednesday through the Day of Pentecost. Volume 3 begins with Trinity Sunday (the First Sunday After Pentecost) and includes all the lessons for June, July, and August. This volume finishes the remainder of the year, including the lessons for All Saints' Day (November 1) and Thanksgiving Day. A new series will then be published for the B Cycle.

A note on language: We have used the term *Old Testament* in this series because that is the language employed by the Consultation on Common Texts, at least up to this point. Pastors and worship committees may wish to consider alternative terms, such as *First Testament* or *Hebrew Scriptures*, that do not imply that those writings somehow have less value than the rest of the Christian Bible. Another option is to refer to *First Lesson* (always from the Hebrew Scriptures), *Second Lesson* (from Acts or the epistles), and *Gospel*.

PREACHING AND WORSHIP AMIDST THE CLASH OF CALENDARS

Perhaps at no other time of the year than in the autumn do preachers and planners of worship experience so many demands on them for attention by diverse kinds of programmatic and special interest concerns. Three calendars are usually competing for attention all the year round, with varying degrees of success at different times.

The most important, of course, is the Christian year calendar itself, which guides us through the varied acts in the drama of our salvation, with commentary provided by the lectionary all along the way. The observance of that calendar and the lectionary keep the Church faithful to the Easter proclamation, since the purpose of the Christian year is to assist us in examining the Easter mystery from different perspectives. The regular return of the Lord's Day reminds us that we are an Easter people, a product of the eighth day of creation, and that through baptism we have been born from above and are now engaged upon a pilgrimage in which we are seeking the things that are above.

The church's programmatic calendar is another significant factor in planning for preaching and worship, particularly in the autumn. For many churches this is the time to swing into action after summer recess. Church school resumes, or if it has not stopped, students now move to different classes. Choirs once more reappear, and it is not unknown for "Back to Church Sunday" to be marked by the donning of vestments or robes that were abandoned after Memorial Day. The denomination as well as the local church uses this time to make special emphases. A pan-Protestant calendar annually observes in the autumn Christian Education Sunday, World Communion Sunday, Laity Sunday, Stewardship Sunday, and National Bible Sunday. Depending upon the particular denomination, one may also be expected to observe Reformation Sunday and United Nations Sunday as well. Homecoming Sunday is regularly observed in autumn by many congregations. Frequently these days come equipped by the denominational program agencies with special orders of service, scripture lessons, and even sermon outlines. Without denying the legitimacy and appropriateness of the interests represented, it may still be said that among American Protestants program Sundays threaten to do to the regular pattern of Christian year and lectionary what the saints days did to the dominical pattern of worship in the medieval church.

The civil calendar is the third contender for the attention of the congregation. In some ways the first of September is the beginning of a new year in the civil calendar. The beginning of school might be said to exercise more influence over the national life than any other single event; so by those dates vacations are planned, houses are bought and sold, clothes are purchased, schedules are arranged. Labor Day weekend is a significant date on many counts, and so it is not unusual to find sermon topics for the Sunday that deal not only with labor but also with beginnings. Election Day and Veterans Day do not appeal as much to a pulpit setting, but it is not unknown for them to become primary themes for the Lord's Day. Perhaps the most difficult issue to deal with in terms of the civil calendar is that of Thanksgiving, because it is so entwined with our national and religious roots. It is easy to forget that Thanksgiving Day is not a day of the Church (eucharistically speaking, for the Church every Sunday is Thanksgiving Day), but is a patriotic occasion dictated by a presidential proclamation. And what the president proclaims is Thanksgiving Day, the fourth Thursday in November, not Thanksgiving Sunday. Yet often a Thanksgiving Sunday is invented so that the people are relieved from the patriotic burden of attending church more than once a week. The Sunday that is thus lost from the Christian year is Christ the King, the very Sunday that allows us to proclaim that we have no time for civil religion and that our citizenship is in heaven!

Because Christianity is incarnational, designed to relate to the world in which we live, all three calendars should be taken seriously. The question becomes one of deciding how Christian preaching and worship relate to the three approaches and by what principles do we set

14

priorities among them. Certain affirmations might be made and regulations established in order to avoid both liturgical chaos and a homiletical pattern that is only a response to squeaking wheels in church or society. For persons who exercise gospel freedom, law is important because it gives us an excuse for breaking it!

1. We affirm the priority of the Lord's Day as the day of the Christian assembly, which meets primarily for the purpose of retelling the story and responding to the story in sacramental actions.

2. We affirm the priority of the lectionary as the primary means by which the story is told and remembered in an orderly and coherent fashion.

3. We affirm the relevance of the scriptures to Christian living as a gift of God. The Bible is not something we have to "make relevant" to our lives, or through which we search to find relevant passages; as the "Word of God" it addresses the depths of our being as we open ourselves to it in earnest prayer and committed study.

4. We affirm the movement from word and sacrament in the assembly to a life of service in the world as the Church becomes God's word and sacrament for the world. Preaching and liturgy lead us to a participation in the sacrificial life of Christ. Christians then have a responsibility to know about the world and its concerns so that our ministry may be both compassionate and informed.

Adherence to these affirmations can help keep the scriptures at the center of the congregation's worship life without using them in a haphazard fashion to serve some purely thematic end. For example, when confronted with the necessity of preaching on Labor Day weekend, the preacher's pattern should not be to decide what he or she thinks about the labor/management issues of the day and then find some umbrella scripture lesson that might relate in a vague way, but need not be referred to at length. In 1993, the first Sunday in September will have the lessons of Proper Eighteen. Two of them offer little help: the Old Testament is the Exodus Passover narrative, and the Gospel is Matthew on maintaining church discipline and order. But the epistle lesson from Romans 13, part of which was heard earlier on the First Sunday in Advent, can now be applied to a different context, that of human labor. What kind of critique of American labor and the marketplace can be offered on the basis of putting on the Lord Jesus Christ and making no provision for the flesh? The issue here is certainly not lack of relevancy of the lectionary passage to the day!

On the other hand, pastors and preachers faced with the ordering of the lessons in 1993 may need to consider some kind of rearranging for World Communion Sunday. Ordinarily the texts for that day would be those of Proper Twenty-two: the Ten Commandments from Exodus, Paul's passionate statement to the Philippians about his desire to know Christ apart from the law, and Matthew's version of the parable of the wicked tenants. None of these lend themselves immediately to a eucharistic exposition without taking the congregation through some convoluted reasoning. There are, however, two alterations to the order of lessons that may serve to relate the day to one of the readings. The Old Testament lessons for Propers Twenty-one and Twenty-two may be alternated. (Since all three lessons are being read in independent sequence, the two are not affected by changing the third. The psalm should be kept in relation to the Old Testament lesson, however.) Proper Twenty-one is the narrative of the water from the rock in the wilderness, a sign of God's care by sustaining the people in the wilderness. This can provide an opportunity for a discussion of the Eucharist as a contemporary sign of God's spiritual nourishment of the Church in the present world. The preacher can emphasize here that the Eucharist is God's action, not ours. Another option is to exchange the Gospel lessons between Propers Twenty-two and Twenty-three. The parable of the wedding banquet (Proper Twenty-three) lends itself more easily to a discussion of the Eucharist as a sign of the Kingdom and the grace of God. In this case, the magnanimity of the king's invitation can be related to World Communion Sunday.

The sequential character of the lessons allows for a seasonal series of sermons; only the preacher's imagination can limit how these may be employed. The Old Testament cycle, which deals with the deliverance of the children of Israel from Egypt through their entrance into the Promised Land and life under the judges, can provide the basis for a series of sermons on what it means for the church to be a pilgrim people, arguing with God in the wilderness of the world, but never being abandoned by God in spite of unfaithfulness and doubt. The epistle lessons explore the life of the church in Philippi and Thessalonica, and they can be expanded to allow for eleven rather than nine Sundays of readings (Propers Eighteen through Twenty-eight), since the individual lessons are not affected by changes within the set. The Last Sunday After Pentecost (Christ the King, Proper Twenty-nine) should, however, keep its own set of lessons to mark the special character of the day. The Gospel lessons are in most cases parables about the Kingdom and its quality of life. A sermon series here can provide the pastor an opportunity to spend the summer "boning up" on the most recent books in social and theological ethics.

As a time of new beginnings, this autumn may also be an opportunity for the preacher to make some New Year's resolutions about preaching. Such resolutions may include fixing a time for study and preparation on one's weekly calendar and keeping to it as inflexibly as one does official board meetings, so that sermon preparation is not relegated to the off-times and the residue of the week. Likewise, disciplined prayer time as preparation for preaching preparation needs to be worked into the schedule. A daily office should be devised by each working pastor as a means of doing the minimal work of prayer, and it should be adhered to whether one likes it or not, because that is what an office is: *officium* a duty. *Look for nothing* magical here, but *a daily office* can be formative for a life in the Spirit that is more than psychological self-help.

The visuals for this long end of the year are green (except when All Saints is celebrated on the first Sunday in November, and then the color is white or gold). Many churches alter the basic green throughout the autumn to move with the changing color of the leaves, picking up more reds and browns and oranges and yellows. Green should still predominate, however, with its suggestion of life and growth.

17

Proper Eighteen
Sunday Between September 4 and 10 Inclusive

Old Testament Texts

Exodus 12:1-14 is one of the central descriptions of how the Passover is to be celebrated and how it functions in the life of Israel. Psalm 149 is a two-sided hymn of praise in which God's ability to destroy and to save is acknowledged.

The Lesson: *Exodus 12:1-14*

The Passover

Setting. The confusion of the present form of Exodus 11–13 confronts any reader with immediate obstacles to interpretation. At least three different traditions have been brought together in these chapters (by at least two different hands) to describe what the salvific power of God is like. These three traditions include the death of the firstborn (Exodus 11, 12:12-13, 29-32; and perhaps 13:1, 11-16), the cultic celebration of Passover (Exodus 12:1-11, 21-27, 43-50), and unleavened bread or massot (Exodus 12:8, 14-20, 34; 13:3-10). It is not the task of a preacher to sort out the complex history of tradition in Exodus 11–13. It is a central task, however, for any interpreter of these texts to raise the question of why these (most likely) originally distinct traditions were brought together; an answer to this question will provide the preacher with an interpretation of what salvation means. The limitation of the Old Testament lesson to Exodus 12:1-14 allows us to narrow the scope of this question to the relationship between Passover and the death of the firstborn; the feast of unleavened bread is not central to these verses—occurring only briefly in v. 8. We aim to determine what salvation means when the death of the firstborn is fused with the tradition of a Passover in Israel.

Structure. The larger structure of Exodus 11–12 accentuates and reinforces the close relationship between the death of the firstborn and Passover. In Exodus 11 God tells Moses that there is yet one final plague that will be brought upon the Egyptians—namely, the death of all firstborn in the land. The reader is told in v. 7 that the result of this plague will be a visible distinction between Egyptians and Israelites. Exodus 12:1-14 immediately follows the divine prediction. In this text, Moses prepares Israel for the night of destruction by telling them how they can be protected from the plague of death. The text can be outlined in the following manner.

    I. The Instructions for the Passover (vv. 1-11)
       A. The time of the Passover
       B. The lamb
       C. The ritual
          1. Kill the lamb at evening
          2. Put blood on doorpost
          3. Eat the lamb in families
          4. Eat in haste
   II. The Interpretation of the Passover (vv. 12-14)
       A. Death of firstborn
       B. The blood-sign for Israel
       C. The memorial

Significance. Questions about the meaning of salvation can best be answered by interpreting the death of the firstborn alone and by showing how the death of the firstborn is transformed when it is linked to the Passover.

First, the death of the firstborn. When read independently, the death of the firstborn is a we-they story, or perhaps better an us-against-them story. The Egyptians are "them," whose firstborn are going to be killed by God, while the Israelites are "us," whose firstborn are going to be alive and well in the morning. This dichotomy is overly simplistic because the reader has been taken through an entire series of plagues in which Pharaoh has had ample time to avoid the plague of death. Nevertheless, the text plunges too quickly toward a resolution when the death of the Egyptian firstborn is read alone, because the distinction between the people of God ("us") and other humans ("them") is something that is rooted in people themselves. It makes much difference in the story about the death of the firstborn if a person's genetic structure is Egyptian or Israelite.

Second, the linking of Passover with death in the story of the firstborn necessarily complicates our understanding of who God is and who the people of God are. First, our understanding of God. If the death of the firstborn gave the impression that God was dangerous only for certain groups of people and that the dangerousness of God was, in fact, in service to the people of God (like a secret weapon), the linking of Passover underscores in no uncertain terms that God is dangerous for all persons, Israelites and Egyptians alike. The Passover instructions make it clear that God's plague of death will not discriminate between ethnic groups, and that only the blood of the lamb will save Israelites. Second, once our understanding of God is complicated with the addition of Passover, then it necessarily follows that our understanding of the people of God will also be changed. By underscoring that God is dangerous for all in the Passover ritual, biblical writers are also saying that any distinction between the people of God and other humans must also lie outside of persons, which is the case in the Passover ritual, where the distinction lies in the sacrificial blood. When Passover is linked to the death of the firstborn the reader learns that Israel is not saved because of ethnicity, or even because they are oppressed, but because they participated in an atoning ritual that covered (or perhaps better, protected) them from the plague of death. Such an understanding of the people of God is implicitly universal, for there is nothing in the story to forbid an Egyptian from seeking the protection of the atoning blood. This insight forces a new reading of Exodus 11:7, for it suggests that only after the event of the death of the firstborn will we know who are the people of God—namely, those whose firstborn have survived because they participated in the atoning ritual.

The story of Passover goes against our modern sensibilities. Although the universal claims of salvation are more popular than ever in the contemporary Church, we frequently root such claims in the belief that Christianity is a better way, and we look in advance at our own cultural (even genetic) setting as proof. The story of Passover argues for the universal claims of God's salvation in an opposite way. The story presents a strong theology of sin in judging both Israel and Egypt (the absence of blood on the doorpost will kill any firstborn), and it is on the basis of this understanding of universal sin that a universal salvation is implied. There is nothing noble about the salvation of the Passover, for the first thing that anyone waking up the next morning must confront is blood dripping in their doorway. There is no idealizing of ones own cultural context here, and the imagery invites reflection on the nature of the Eucharist for Christians.

The Response: *Psalm 149*

A Call to Praise

Setting. Psalm 149 is a hymn of praise that evolves into a call for the worshiping community to participate in a holy war against the nations. The language of holy war takes center stage in vv. 7-9*a* where the faithful are called to wreak vengeance on nations, to bind kings, and to execute judgment.

Structure. Psalm 149 separates into two parts that can be outlined in the following manner.

    I. A Call to Sing a New Song (vv. 1-4)
        A. Call to praise (vv. 1-3)
        B. Reason for praise (v. 4)
    II. A Call to Praise God and Participate in Holy War (vv. 5-9*a*)
        A. Call to praise (vv. 5-6)
        B. Call to holy war (vv. 7-9*a*)
   III. Conclusion (v. 9*b*)

Significance. Psalm 149 has strong undercurrents of holy war, which suggests that it is a "we-they" psalm. The people of God are clearly contrasted to the nations and encouraged to defeat and destroy them. This strong theme of holy war has often left modern interpreters uncomfortable because of its apparent lack of regard for all of humanity. Three comments are necessary in the light of this reservation. First, the psalm is clear that, indeed, boundaries do exist between the people of God and all humanity in general. In an age of increasing globalization, where boundaries become more and more unclear, the confession of this hymn—that to be the people of God is not one choice among many, but a qualitatively new existence—is a message that must be celebrated in our contemporary worship. Second, the linking of Passover and death of the firstborn in Exodus 11–12 provides a strong reminder that the boundaries between the people of God and all of humanity do not rest in persons, but in the activity of God. In fact, if we were to interpret Psalm 149 only in the light of the Passover, then the holy war that is called for in vv. 7-9*a* would be participation in the atoning blood of the lamb. Third, the focus of Psalm 149 is on the salvific activity of God and the assurance that God will achieve divine ends. This security is praiseworthy in Psalm 149.

New Testament Texts

The sequential reading of Romans and Matthew brings us to consider two passages that deal in very practical terms with matters of daily life. Yet, both passages teach that in everyday situations Christians are called to distinctive behavior.

The Epistle *Romans 13:8-14*

Love and Its Eschatological Motivation

Setting. The lesson comes from a section of Romans in which Paul offers practical advice about matters of everyday living, which is distinctively Christian. It is noteworthy that the concluding verses of the lesson have a pronounced eschatological cast. By emphasizing the eschatological language and concern of 13:11-14, we clarify the context of Paul's remarks in 13:8-10. All that Paul thought and all that Paul taught was qualified by his belief that Judgment Day was at hand.

Structure. There are two parts to the lesson, vv. 8-10 and vv. 11-14. The first section stresses the necessity of love as the essence of Christian life; the second declares the eschatological motivation of Christian love. The correlation of these two elements in the lesson points up the dynamic that should inform the use of this lesson for preaching. This is an urgent message, not merely another recycled pitch for morality!

Significance. The plain sense of this passage is fairly straightforward: Christians are to act decently, and more, they are to live lives of love. God's promised judgment in Jesus Christ makes a life of love not only prudent but necessary. Nevertheless, there are plenty of ways to squander the life that God has given us—namely by living dishonorably, in pursuit of selfish but destructive pleasure. Yet Christians are called to a different way of life—one made not only possible but real in the Lord Jesus Christ.

The call to a life of love is a call away from certain kinds of behavior. It is a call out of darkness and into light. Thus as believers we do not merely define our lives in negative terms—all the things that we do not do. Rather, we turn away from the ignoble to embrace and actualize a godly manner of living. This call to new life in Christ is both urgent and powerful. Every moment counts, for indeed each moment may well be our last. Yet we are not merely given marching orders; we are given a vital relationship to our living Lord Jesus Christ, and that relationship ensures that we can live in the noble fashion to which God calls us. The reality of Christian life is essentially christological, not merely moral. We live out God's love, not out of a rule book; and it is Christ who calls, directs, and energizes our living and loving. Paul's metaphor is that we "put on the Lord Jesus Christ." The image is striking and suggestive. Even superficial advocates of high fashion argue that "the clothes make the person," meaning that a suit or dress can "define" one in the eyes of others.

Strikingly, to put on Christ is to give definition to ourselves, especially in relation to others. As we wear Christ, we bear Christ, and in a very real sense, we are Christ in relation to others. As we wrap ourselves in Jesus Christ, he takes charge of our lives for his good purposes. Indeed, this is the mystical dimension of Christian faith, which too often we leave unfulfilled.

Furthermore, we must consider the meaning of a life of love. In our world the word *love* is used so often and so loosely that it holds no meaning (except on a tennis court!). We love everything from green beans to baseball to jogging to holding hands. But what does it mean "to love"? We may attempt to define love, offering definitions that are appropriately active and necessarily more than emotional—for example, to will the well-being of others, even at a cost to ourselves. But, even if accurate, such definitions remain flatly abstract. For a genuinely Christian definition of love, we have to look to the person of our Lord Jesus Christ. A look at him gives definition to love. Jesus lived his life for others in obedience to God's will. He did not spend his life for the glory of blazing martyrdom; rather, he sacrificed his life for the accomplishment of God's purposes in relation to the salvation of others. Thus, in our world, love is the outcome of obedience to God's will. When we are clothed in love as Paul suggests, we "put on the Lord Jesus Christ, and make no provision for the flesh, to gratify its desires" (11:14).

The Gospel: *Matthew 18:15-20*

Conflict Resolution, Authority, and Responsible Prayer

Setting. The lesson comes in the latter portion of the fourth major section of Matthew's presentation of Jesus' ministry, where Jesus is busy teaching his disciples what it means to be the Church. The teaching combines admonitions and warnings. Our lesson follows Jesus' parable of the lost sheep, a text that reveals both God's desire to recover those who are "lost" and God's joy over finding them. With God's ways made plain, our lesson turns to the responsibilities of Christians for several dimensions of Church life.

25

Structure. The lesson, composed of six verses, has three distinguishable parts. First, vv. 15-17 give instructions for settling disputes among believers. Second, v. 18 issues a statement about Christians' authority for "binding and loosing." And third, vv. 19-20 speak of the efficacy of corporate Christian prayer. One may attend to only one or two parts, but there is an advantage in holding the sections together as will be seen below.

Significance. Verses 15-17 articulate a code of Christian conduct concerning the resolution of conflicts between (or, by extrapolation among) members of congregations. Every member of every church should read these words regularly, so that leaders and laity alike should always insist that controversies be settled according to these directions. This is not to say that scripture is merely a rulebook, but when we come across teaching as sane and sound as this, we should be eager to comply. Think of disasters you have known or heard about in the life of congregations and ask yourself whether things would not have turned out quite differently if Jesus' directions had been carefully followed.

Jesus' words set forth a means of dealing with disagreements that blends and balances love and justice. The call to live as the God who pursues and rejoices over the finding of the lost is not a call to a mushy compassion that simply lets anything go. Christians are called to recognize right and wrong in love. Thus the first step in attempting to accomplish reconciliation when we are at odds with others is a private move, designed to avoid the magnification of difficulties by casting the problem into the public arena where self-defensive self-righteousness can easily lunge to the fore. Moreover, in this directive Jesus recognized that if there are differences between us, the responsibility to work for a resolution lies on us, and since Jesus' words envision two believers at odds with each other, the responsibility is mutual. But what if nothing comes of our best efforts? We do not leave the matter there, for we are directed to broaden our efforts by including one or two others who can both moderate and witness the matter. If there is still no resolution, Jesus directs us to go to the whole church (recall that first-century congregations were naturally smaller than many of our modern mega-churches!). The purpose of delivering the matter to the congregation is still for the achievement of reconciliation. But finally, if the recalcitrant member refuses the urgings of the church, he or she is to be regarded as one outside the church. Jesus' words here seem harsh, "let such a one be to you as a Gentile and a tax collector." Yet, if we ponder the words for a moment, we will recall two things: (1) Gentiles and tax collectors were recognizably outside the Church, but (2) they were the very ones whom God pursued in order to bring them into the Church. The offending member is not being simply dismissed, but rather the matter has run its human course and is now being given completely to God. Offenders are dealt with, but ultimately in love and for the purposes of reconciliation. Final authority in such matters rests with God.

Verse 18 records words to the Church that are strikingly similar to the words spoken by Jesus to Peter in Matthew 16:19. Generally the sense of the statements is the same. There are responsibilities inherent in discipleship. Jesus charges the Church to exercise the authority for doing the work of God on this earth. The Church does not play God, but being disciples means that we are to exercise the power of God for the doing of God's will. This verse should probably be read in relation to the foregoing verses as a kind of confirmation of the difficult decision to regard a member of the congregation as no longer a member of the Church.

In turn, vv. 19-20 recognize that we are to be responsible in our prayers. This promise from Jesus is not the equivalent of a Christian wishing-well with guaranteed results. Historically many such prayers have gone unanswered, possibly an indication that the agreement among the people was a bad one or that the gathering was Christless, but perhaps this most indicates that Jesus' words were simply misunderstood. In fact, it may be unwise to read these verses out of their context where they are related to winning back a lost member (18:15-17) and to the responsibility to be faithful in forgiving (18:21-22).

Proper Eighteen: The Celebration

An emphasis on today's Old Testament lesson will remind us that we are an Easter people, celebrating the Christian Passover on each Lord's Day. The following hymn by Charles Wesley will help make the "Easter connection" with our celebration of Sunday and the last stanza will whisper of applications to the civil Labor Day observance. St. Catherine or Sussex Carol are tunes which will fit well.

> Come, let us with our Lord arise,
> Our Lord, who made both earth and skies:
> Who died to save the world he made,
> And rose triumphant from the dead;
> He rose, the Prince of life and peace,
> And stamped the day for ever his.
>
> This is the day the Lord has made,
> That all may see his love displayed,
> May feel his resurrection's power,
> And rise again, to fall no more,
> In perfect righteousness renewed,
> And filled with all the life of God.
>
> Then let us render him his own,
> With solemn prayer approach his throne,
> With meekness hear the gospel word,
> With thanks his dying love record,
> Our joyful hearts and voices raise,
> And fill his courts with songs of praise.
>
> Honor and praise to Jesus pay
> Throughout his consecrated day;
> Be all in Jesus' praise employed,
> Nor leave a single moment void;
> With utmost care the time improve,
> And only breathe his praise and love.

Notice in the third stanza the subtle connection of word and sacrament: "hear the gospel word" and "with thanks [Eucharist] his dying love record."

Funeral scenes in Egyptian tombs frequently depict the eldest son making offerings for the soul of the deceased father. Some scholars maintain that only the eldest son could perform this salvific rite, and so the loss of the Egyptian firstborn was a double tragedy, because not only was the earthly future made insecure, the heavenly one was also cast into doubt. The preacher may wish to explore this in terms of the christological reversal in which it is the death of the only-begotten that brings life to all in the Christian Pasch. This might also be a time to discuss blood imagery and its importance in understanding salvation theology.

Should the preacher choose not to deal with the theme of labor in the sermon today, the prayers and intercessions ought to reflect concern for both workers and the unemployed, for management and working conditions, and for various types of work. A litany can incorporate mention of the various ways members of the congregation are employed and the contributions they make to the common good. The *Presbyterian Worshipbook* contains a large selection of prayers for those in various occupations which can serve as a model for the planning committee. Members might be encouraged to attend service in whatever work clothes are appropriate to their jobs.

Proper Nineteen
Sunday Between September 11 and 17 Inclusive

Old Testament Texts

Exodus 14:19-31 is the account of how God rescued Israel from the Egyptians at the Reed Sea. Exodus 15:1*b*-11, 20-21 is a hymn that celebrates this event, and it is sometimes said to be the oldest text in the Bible.

The Lesson: *Exodus 14:19-31*

Rescue at the Sea

Setting. Few would disagree with the statement that the Exodus event is the central story of salvation in the Old Testament. Problems of interpretation arise, however, when we ask just what happened in the Exodus event, for it encompasses a sequence of stories. The announcement of the death of the Egyptian firstborn and the protective ritual of the Passover in Exodus 11–13, which were the focus of interpretation last week, are part of the Exodus event, but they are not the whole story of what salvation means. The Exodus also includes the story of Israel's divine rescue at the Reed Sea in Exodus 14–15, which is the focus of study for this week.

The central question for interpretation is an extension of the question that was raised last week—namely, what salvation meant when the death of the firstborn was linked with the Passover ritual. We concluded that the linking of these two stories underscored how the atonement of the blood of the lamb was potentially universal for all humankind. The question this week is to determine what salvation means when the death of the firstborn and the Passover (Exodus 11–13) are linked with the divine rescue of Israel at the Reed Sea (Exodus 14–15).

Structure. Exodus 14:19-31 describes the confrontation between Yahweh and Pharaoh at the Reed Sea. After the Passover and death of the firstborn, Israel is driven out of Egypt by the Egyptians in Exodus 12:33-36, which introduces the motif of journeying that has not been part of the Exodus story up to this point. Israel is now on the move, and the geographical notices in Exodus 13:17-21; 14:1-4 underscore that their travels are extensive and that they are the result of God's leading. This is important information for interpreting Exodus 14:19-31. The confrontation at the Reed Sea is part of a larger story in which Israel is journeying with God. The story should not be read as a chance meeting between a fleeing band of slaves and the Egyptian army but as an event that is being orchestrated by God. The outline of the story illustrates clearly the central role of God at the Reed Sea.

    I. Divine Protection (vv. 19-20)
    II. Divine Salvation of Israel through the Water (vv. 21-25)
    III. Divine Destruction of Egypt in the Water (vv. 26-29)
    IV. Summary (vv. 30-31)

Significance. The story of God's action at the Reed Sea in Exodus 14:19-31 requires an interpretation in isolation, and then the Reed Sea event must be interpreted in conjunction with the atoning death of the firstborn during the Passover.

First, the Reed Sea event. The confrontation at the Reed Sea is a story about God; it is not a story about Israel or even about Egypt. The central point of the story is that the salvific power of God is reliable and that consequently the people of God can be secure in the belief that God will indeed protect them. The reliablility of God's salvation is explored on two levels in the telling of the story, both historically and cosmologically. The confrontation between God and Pharaoh and the ultimate destruction of the Egyptian army in the sea explores the power of God's salvation in history. When the story is read on this level, it provides a strong message about the limitation of human power and how hubris cannot stop the salvation of God no matter how strong it may appear. This message is a repetition of the opening chapters, where the power of Pharaoh was also thwarted by what appeared to be the powerless midwives and the Levitical mother of Moses, who were acting as God agents (see Proper Sixteen).

The confrontation at the sea is also a cosmological story. On this level it explores the power of God's salvation far beyond any human potential. Thus, when read in this way, Pharaoh and the Egyptian army recede into the background as the opponents of God, and they are replaced by the sea itself. In ancient Israel the sea nearly took on divine status because it symbolized the divine power of chaos. The sea evoked the breakdown of all structure, and thus it was the ultimate opponent of God. In Canaanite religion the sea was in fact a God named Yamm, who represented chaotic power in this world. In Exodus 14:19-31, however, notice how the sea becomes a mere tool in God's hands to the point where Israelites can actually walk through the middle of this chaos without even getting their feet wet. As a cosmological story, the Reed Sea event is a strong proclamation that God's salvation is absolutely reliable even when opposed by evil divine powers.

Second, if we wish to interpret the whole story of salvation, then we must interpret Israel's divine rescue at the Reed Sea in the larger context of the Passover. What does salvation mean when these stories are linked together? The Passover is a story that takes place almost outside of time. It occurs during the sunless, timeless hours of the night, and there is no real plot. Instead it requires participation in a ritual that protects and thus transforms people. The central role of the ritual in this story conveys the message that the power of the Passover is always present and thus constantly available for its participants. It is an eternal sacrament. By placing the account of Israel's divine rescue at the Reed Sea in the larger context in which Israel is following God, biblical writers merge the sacramental power of the Passover with

Israel's ongoing historical life. The linking of the Passover and the event at the Reed Sea is a strong statement that the salvation of God experienced in atonement (Passover) inevitably propels the people of God on a journey in which they must follow God, and live only by God's protection (Reed Sea). This journey requires faith, and it is to this topic that the story turns in the closing summary of Exodus 14:30-31, when the reader is told that Israel believed in God and in Moses.

The Response: *Exodus 15:1b-11, 20-21*

Celebrating God's Salvation at the Reed Sea

Setting. The narrative version of the event at the Reed Sea is, for purposes of lectionary-based preaching, reinterpreted in an antiphonal song, led by brother and sister, Moses and Miriam. Some scripture scholars, however, have suggested that this poetic, hymnic celebration of the event is actually older than the narrative distillation in Exodus 14; in fact it may be the oldest written text that was edited into the Hebrew Bible. Exodus 15:1b-11 (and continuing on to v. 18) is a stunning, vivid exaltation of God's power, as understood by Moses. Exodus 15:20-21 is preceded by a tidbit of narrative transition (v. 19) and includes a narrative introduction (v. 20) that explains how Miriam and all the women of Israel sang a hymn of praise to God immediately after Israel's divine rescue at the Reed Sea. Note that the song sung by the women is nearly identical to the first verse in the men's part (15:1b), so that v. 21 may have functioned as a chorus.

Structure. The chorus of Miriam in Exodus 15:21 consists of two couplets, which include a call to praise and the reason for praise.

> Sing to the LORD,
> for he has triumphed gloriously;
> the horse and his rider
> he has thrown into the sea.

The verses sung by Moses and the men begin with the same two couplets, and then proceed antiphonally with Yahweh and Pharaoh as alternate subjects in the pattern.

34

I. Yahweh's Strength as Divine Warrior (vv. 2-3)
II. Pharoah's Drowning (vv. 4-5)
III. Yahweh's Power Over the Sea (vv. 6-8)
IV. The Enemy's Aggression (v. 9)
V. Yahweh Sinks Them Like Lead (v. 10)

Verses 11 and 12 close the doxology by recounting how God ordered the earth to swallow the Egyptian enemies.

Significance. This hymn and its chorus celebrate God's salvation both in the context of history and in the larger realm of the cosmos, as was the case in Exodus 14:19-31. The Song of Moses and Miriam celebrates the gift of salvation as a reversal of the power structures in this world. God is worthy of praise in this song because God stopped the Egyptians, who were the oppressors. God's salvation is also seen as a defeat of the chaotic waters. Rhetorically the hymnist asserts that no other god, even Yamm, can compete with the wonder and splendor of God's sovereignty over the physical characteristics of this world (earth and sea) or God's dominion over the human enemies who try to thwart the freedom of the people of God.

New Testament Texts

The lesson from Romans works to establish the basis of Christians accepting other believers who are markedly different in their patterns of piety. The reading from Matthew takes up the theme of forgiveness, making the point that we are to be boundless and Godlike in extending grace to others.

The Epistle: *Romans 14:1-12*

Acceptable Despite Real Differences

Setting. The lesson for this Sunday comes in the larger section of Paul's practical advice to the Roman believers (Romans 12-15). These verses take up a new matter—namely, how to live with the marked differences in practices of piety among members of the congregation. While at a glance chapter 14 seems capable of standing alone, we should observe that Paul's teaching in this passage comes immediately after his eschatological pronouncement in 13:11-14; so that the sense of his comments is colored by the eschatological hues of his thinking.

Structure. The material in the lesson is a kind of spiraling, progressive argument. Verses 1-4 take up differences over diet among the Romans. Then, vv. 5-6 mix the matter of calendar observance with the issue of eating. In turn, vv. 7-9 make a christological statement about common Christian existence; and finally, vv. 10-12 amplify the argument by stating Paul's point theologically.

Significance. In a nutshell Paul says differences in religious practices are not matters that ought to divide believers. Paul recognizes and allows certain differences in styles of piety, but he argues that these should not fragment a community that has been united by faith in one Lord.

The preacher confronting this text faces a challenge. The concrete issues addressed in the passage are highly time conditioned—diet and calendar as divisive religious issues—so that some kind of analogy building is required for the text to live today. But, the temptation to find and use analogies may cause one to move too quickly and miss the issue lying behind the practices that Paul mentions. Thus it is worth the time to come to terms with this text historically and theologically, so that the sermon may indeed be related to the sense of the lesson and not merely matters touched on in the text.

First, vv. 1-4 speak of those who are "weak in faith." Apparently these are persons who eat only vegetables because they find the consumption of meat problematic. Paul addressed a similar issue in I Corinthians 8, and in part an awareness of the Corinthian problem assists us in making sense of the text in Romans 14. In the first-century, in pagan contexts, much of the meat sold in the market came from the pagan temple cults where animals were offered to the pagan gods. Not all meat was from the pagan temples, but the chance was always there that meat had been devoted originally to some god(s). Some early Christians were bothered by the association of the meat with the "false gods"; some were not. For those who cared, the only safe option was to avoid meat altogether. "Weak in faith" in Romans most likely names those whose religious scruples led them to abstain from meat. Notice in the context of our lesson that Paul does not call those who ate meat "strong in faith"; rather, he reserves that phrase until 15:1. Also, notice that the issues addressed in I Corinthians and Romans are different! In I Corinthians the controversy was over whether one should or should not eat the meat offered to idols, but in Romans the matter at the heart of Paul's discussion is that of accepting fellow Christians with whom one has recognizable differences. Paul tells "those who eat" not to despise or judge those who do not eat, for those not eating are the Lord's and the matter rests with the Lord. Moreover, even if their scruples demonstrate a weakness in faith, the Lord "is able to make them stand," that is God has the power to overcome their weakness and justify them.

Verses 5-6 make the matter more complex by introducing calendar observance, the practice of piety in prescribed ways and at prescribed times. But the point here is the same as in vv. 1-4—God is over all believers despite their differences, so that they are united in the Lord. The implication of Paul's remarks is that, therefore, the believers should recognize and celebrate their unity in the Lord, not focus on differences in practices.

Verses 7-9 make a christological statement about the common core of Christian life. All Christians have one Lord, the Lord of life and death. The bond that holds believers together despite their differences is the death and Resurrection of Jesus Christ, which claims them and unites them in life and death. Verses 10-12 continue this line of argumentation by making a pronounced theological statement against the judgment of one group of Christians by another. The ultimate authority for judging believers belongs to God. Paul proves this point with quotations of Isaiah 49:18 and 45:23. Christians stand united before the God who justifies them all despite their real differences. If this is God's way, then, Paul declares, it must be ours! Therefore, we accept one another despite the differences. Acceptance has a theological basis, not merely a practical one.

The Gospel: *Matthew 18:21-35*

Divine Forgiveness from the Heart

Setting. The theme of forgiveness, implicit in the earlier verses of last week's lesson, becomes explicit in the passage for this Sunday. These verses are the last substantive portion of the fourth major section of Matthew's presentation of Jesus' ministry where Jesus instructs the disciples about what it means to be the church.

Structure. The text falls cleanly into two related parts, though the longer second section of the lesson itself can be seen in smaller units. First, vv. 21-22 recount a conversation between Peter and Jesus that sets up the parable in the rest of the lesson. Second, v. 35 records the parable of the unforgiving servant. The parable proper runs from v. 23 through v. 34, and v. 35 is a kind of tag line that applies one sense of the parable to the hearers/readers as a pointed warning.

Significance. Matthew has Peter turn to Jesus upon hearing Jesus' teachings about the way in which believers are to settle their differences in the context of the life of the Church. Matthew connects the verses of this week's lesson to the foregoing material with the word *then*. Thus there is a relationship between the need for reconciliation and the need for forgiveness. True reconciliation comes through forgiveness, not merely through excusing others. It means giving up our rightful resentment, not merely agreeing to regard others as innocent, whether they are guilty or not. Implicit in Matthew's connection of these passages is the crucial spiritual lesson that true reconciliation means the elimination of wrath.

Thus, it should come as no surprise that even when Peter states a standard of mercy that was unprecedented, Jesus calls for more. The mind of the time held that persons could be forgiven one, two, and even three times, but not four times. Peter grasped enough of Jesus' teachings to see that the call to a higher righteousness makes old standards inadequate, so he tests his insight by asking Jesus whether seven times are enough. To Peter's credit, he did expand the idea of forgiveness 133 percent; but he is still thinking in terms of measurable mercy, not unlimited grace. Jesus calls Peter beyond a calculating approach to forgiveness by multiplying Peter's seven. Readers of the NRSV will immediately notice that the translators read Jesus' words as "seventy-seven" rather than the traditional "seventy times seven." The decision to alter the text is debatable, but given either reading the sense of Jesus' statement is the same. Forgiveness is not arithmetic, and we are called to forgive freely from the heart, not begrudgingly from the head.

Then comes the parable. This rather long story starts with the telltale parabolic beginning, "the kingdom of heaven may be compared to. . . ." Yet, there is little in the story that is enigmatic or strange. Only the amount of the king's servant's debt, about 150,000 years' wages, is peculiar; and this simply establishes the magnitude of the obligation. The rest of the story gives a pretty clear lesson—so clear, in fact, that the preacher will be strangely tempted to turn the parable into a moral lesson rather than a declaration of gospel. Indeed, one way of reading the closing line (v. 35) will provide even further temptation to treat the parable like an Aesop's fable.

Yet, notice what Jesus says in v. 35. It is not that we better forgive others or God will get us. No, Jesus says God's wrath will come on those who do not "forgive [their] brother or sister from [their] hearts." It is the genuineness of the forgiveness, not merely the act of excusing that concerns Jesus. But, how can we do more than try to live out the call to forgiveness? How can we possibly guarantee that our forgiveness will be from the heart?

At base level this parable, as v. 35 makes clear, is about the true experience of grace. God is a God of grace. Like the king in the story, God has compassion on our human failures, and like the king, God acts even more graciously than we could ever expect. The servant who owed an impossible debt simply asked for more time to pay what he owed, but the king compassionately and graciously forgave the debt! When we experience such grace, truly, we are transformed in gratitude. Grace that is experienced as grace, in turn, begets grace. If

God's grace has affected our lives, we will live differently in relation to others. This transformation through the experience of grace is not something mechanical or mathematical, rather it comes "from the heart."

Proper Nineteen: The Celebration

As last week's Old Testament lesson provided an opportunity to reflect again on the meaning of Sunday in relation to the Easter event, so today's lesson allows us to think about the meaning of baptism in relation to Christian living. The crossing of the Reed Sea is connected in the liturgy to Easter Eve with its reading of that narrative and the administration of baptism. Now, at the beginning of September, we have some leisure in which to think back on that event and examine in deeper ways its consequences for our lives and witness. The two Sundays allow us to dissect the Paschal mystery into two parts for closer examination.

The crossing of the Reed Sea is the story of the creation of a nation, and for the next few weeks in the liturgy we will be tracing the history of that nation's formation in the desert. They were not created a perfect people. In baptism we are also a new creation, but we are not a perfect people and are always in the process of growing into our baptisms as we learn what it means to put on Christ. Both the epistle and the Gospel lessons are examples of what it means to be growing into Christian maturity. Paul deals with various types of Christian one-upmanship in Rome, and Peter seeks to prove his own worthiness by his ability to forgive. As the commentary makes clear, we deal not with a moralizing tale but rather with an expression of the radical grace of God. Only that grace can make us anew in baptism; only that grace can work a change in the way we treat others, when we realize how grace has affected us.

Liturgically, this approach to the lessons may lead naturally into an act of renewing baptismal vows. The Old Testament lesson may also provide the scriptural warrant for the administration of baptism on this day. Easter hymns that would be appropriate on this September Sunday for relating to baptism are "The Day of Resurrection" and

"Christ Is Alive! Let Christians Sing." If the Eucharist is celebrated, "Christ Is Risen! Shout Hosanna!" (*The United Methodist Hymnal,* no. 307) is also appropriate. The gospel hymn, "I Serve a Risen Savior," would be a fitting concluding hymn.

The Gospel lesson, with its emphasis on forgiving one another, suggests the use of one of the formulas of confession that involves confessing to one another as well as to God. Here is one such form.

L: Let us confess our sins before God and one another.

P: Gracious God:
we confess to you
and to our fellow members in the Body of Christ
that we have sinned in thought, word and deed,
and in what we have failed to do.
Forgive us our sins,
and deliver us from the power of evil,
for the sake of your Son who died for us,
Jesus Christ our Lord.

L: In the name of Christ you are forgiven.

P: In the name of Christ you are forgiven.

Proper Twenty
Sunday Between September 18 and 24 Inclusive

Old Testament Texts

Exodus 16:2-15 is the account of how Israel was miraculously fed manna by God in the wilderness. Psalm 105:1-6, 37-45 is a hymn that praises God who cares for Israel on the wilderness journey.

The Lesson: *Exodus 16:2-15*

Grace Cannot Be Stored Up

Setting. We observe two background features when interpreting the miracle of manna in Exodus 16:2-15. First, it is important to see that the larger literary setting of this story is a journey. The motif of journeying with God links all of the wilderness stories with the Exodus. These stories are an extension of the conclusion that was reached last week in our interpretation of the divine rescue at the Reed Sea—namely, that atonement inevitably propels the people of God on a faith journey. This insight provides a strong argument for including the itinerary notice in Exodus 16:1 in the lectionary text, for it underscores the motif of journeying. Second, the setting has shifted in Exodus 16 from Egypt and its outer boundaries to the wilderness itself. Israel is no longer fleeing from Pharaoh as was the case at the Reed Sea, and the absence of this motif allows us to focus more sharply on the quality of Israel's faith in following God on this journey. As a result, the primary conflict in Exodus 16 is not between

God and some other power (either Pharaoh or the sea) in order to determine who will have control over Israel. Rather, the conflict is in the people of God themselves, and it concerns the question of whether or not they have the faith to follow God.

Structure. The lectionary text must be expanded in two directions. It should, for reasons stated above, include v. 1 and continue at least through v. 21. In v. 4 God replies to Israel's complaint concerning the lack of food (vv. 2-3) by stating that bread will be miraculously supplied from heaven and that this gift of grace would be a test for Israel. As a story of testing Exodus 16 must include Israel's response to the manna, which requires that the reading be extended at least through v. 21.

    I. The Threat of the Wilderness Journey and Israel's Complaint (vv. 1-3)
   II. The Divine Response and Test (vv. 4-12)
      A. Announcement: Gift of bread as test (v. 4)
      B. Instructions (vv. 5-12)
      C. The gift and its interpretation (vv. 13-19)
  III. Israel's Failure (vv. 20-21)

The present structure of the chapter includes at least two different stories, which have not been harmonized completely in the editing of the text. The two stories become evident when we note that even though the central focus of the story is on the manna in the morning, there is also an additional motif about meat being provided in the evening. Furthermore, by ending the story at v. 21 we have cut off one of the central purposes of the story in its present form, which is to tie the gift of manna into Sabbath worship in vv. 22-30. We will return to this point at the end of the section on significance.

Significance. The gift of manna in the wilderness is a story of grace. Israel is threatened by starvation, and God responds with bread from heaven. This is certainly the central message if the story is stopped at v. 15, as it presently is in the lectionary. Yet this simplistic reading of the text will force closure or resolution too quickly, for these biblical writers have qualifications to add on the subject of grace, especially when trying to avoid a self-centered understanding of personal favors granted by God. In particular the text shows how grace must shape the lives of the people of God. This point is made through the addition of specific instructions about when the manna must be collected and eaten, and it is the instructions that become the test for Israel. The central instruction is that the manna cannot be saved or stored up, but must be received anew every morning. This instruction raises the question of whether Israel will have the faith to live solely by the grace of God's gift from heaven—which will mean taking only as much food as they need each day—or will they try to horde manna. They opt for the latter in v. 20, and thus they *fail* the test. Yet, paradoxically, there is no security in what appeared to be the safer choice, because the manna rots at the end of the day.

The preacher could emphasize that God's grace cannot be stored up, and that if we try to horde it for ourselves, we make it foul and thus turn grace into something rotten. Grace must be claimed anew every day. It does not earn interest, and it cannot be stored up for personal manipulation. This means of receiving grace anew each day is the test for the people of God.

The story of God's grace has a further point if we extend the narrative to the end of Exodus 16. In the present form of the text, the story of manna now functions as a prelude to a very strong statement about Sabbath worship. By tying the miracle of manna with worship, biblical writers are pushing this wilderness story into the present time. Their point is that Israel's daily gift of manna in the wilderness is much like God's continuing gift of worship. Like manna, worship is a divine gift that is central to the life of faith, which cannot be stored up, but must be sought anew, regularly.

The Response: *Psalm 105:1-6, 37-45*

A Song of Praise

Setting. The psalm for this Sunday is the last of three entries from Psalm 105. Psalm 105:1-6 [7-15], 16-22 was used on Proper

Fourteen, in conjunction with the story of Joseph and his brothers, and Psalm 105:[1-6] 23-26 was used on Proper Seventeen, in conjunction with the call of Moses in Exodus 3:1-15. Psalm 105:1-6, 37-45 completes the praise of salvation history by recounting the wilderness period and gift of the land. See the entry for Proper Fourteen for introductory commentary on vv. 1-6 for the psalm.

Structure. The inclusion of vv. 1-6 (as was the case in Propers Fourteen and Seventeen) aids in anchoring vv. 37-45 more clearly in praise, which can be divided into three parts.

I. God's Leading Israel from Egypt (vv. 37-38)
II. God's Leading Israel in the Wilderness (vv. 39-41)
III. God's Gift of the Land (vv. 42-45)

Significance. Covenant is the central theme of vv. 37-45. According to v. 42 God saved Israel from Egypt, led them through the wilderness, and gave them the gift of the land because God is bound by a previous promise to Abraham: "For he remembered his holy promise, and Abraham his servant." This verse refers to the covenant with Abraham that was spelled out in vv. 8-11 and provided an introduction to the events of salvation history. For the psalmist, salvation history is the result of God's commitment to covenant. Because of this fact, the mere recounting of Israel's past blessing will inevitably lead to divine praise.

Psalm 105:37-45 provides helpful commentary on Exodus 16 in two ways. First, with its sweeping confession of how God saved Israel from Egypt, led them through the wilderness, and gave them the land, it underscores the point made earlier, of how the story of manna is part of a much larger journey. Second, the focus on God throughout these verses (note how nearly every verse begins with "He [God] led, spread, opened, remembered") provides a larger context for interpreting Israel's test of faith in Exodus 16. In particular, the sweeping panorama in vv. 37-45 of God's gracious activity throughout salvation history encourages the reader not to hoard grace selfishly as though it were a scarce commodity, but to look for it anew each day. The evidence of God's grace is everywhere to be praised.

New Testament Texts

The reading from Philippians reminds us that things are not always as they seem, especially if we try viewing them from a theological point of view. And, the parable in Matthew spins a telling story about who God really is and who we all too often are.

The Epistle: *Philippians 1:21-30*

Another Way of Looking at Life

Setting. We first encountered Philippians as the epistle lesson for the Liturgy of the Passion in Year A. The following discussion of setting is in part a repetition of the entry for the Sixth Sunday in Lent.

The Philippian congregation was the first European church founded by Paul, and it was one with which he maintained a very positive relationship. He was in prison at the time he penned this letter, and he seems to have written for several reasons: (1) to thank the Philippians for their support, physical and spiritual; (2) to discuss Epaphroditus' visit to him in behalf of the Philippians; and (3) to address difficulties and potential problems in the life of the church. The lesson comes early in the body of the letter (1:12–3:21). Paul initially mentioned and discussed the positive value of his imprisonment at the time he was writing. Then, our lesson discusses Paul's likely fate and the meaning of certain hardships that the Philippians are experiencing.

Structure. There are two recognizable sections to the verses in the lesson. First, vv. 21-26 are a subsection of a larger unit, 1:19-26, in which Paul explicates his fortune and expresses his conviction that whatever may happen to him will be for the good, whether that is life or death. Second, vv. 27-30 form a distinct unit of thought and initiate a series of exhortations advocating Christian unity, which continue through 2:18.

Significance. Paul begins in vv. 21-25 by identifying the options that lie before him as he faces apparently grave charges: He is either going to continue living, or he is going to die. At a glance one of these outcomes certainly appears preferable to the other. Yet surprisingly, Paul does not see matters this way. His living relationship with the Lord Jesus Christ is so real, that he shows no fear of death. This does not mean that he is eager to go down in a blaze of martyrdom (Paul is not Ignatius!). Rather, he lives out a vital involvement with Christ, who has died but is now raised. Thus Paul can view death as more than the end of his life; indeed, he can say, "dying is gain." This is not a romantic appreciation of death. Death is not good. But death does not have the final word; Christ does. Paul understands that the risen Lord can use even the handiwork of the final enemy, death (see I Corinthians 15:26), to God's own good ends. In death the current distance between Paul and his Lord will be eliminated.

Paul continues, however, by stating his conviction that he will be released from prison and will continue living for the sake of the Philippians. While he understands that his death would be good for himself, his continuing life would be an opportunity for service. Paul's belief that he will be released seems based on his understanding of his vocation as a calling to service, not privilege. The life we live as Christians is to be dominantly a life of service. The gift of life is not simply something to savor; it is something to be spent in behalf of others. With his mind on future service, in v. 26, Paul expresses his intention to come to the Philippians after being released from prison "for [their] progress and joy in the faith" (v. 25).

In vv. 27-30 Paul moves in a new direction, admonishing the Philippians to Christian unity. Perhaps extending the pattern of thought observed in vv. 21-26, Paul now reminds the Philippians that their own situation in life is an opportunity for service to Christ. The lives of the Philippians are to be profound testimony to the freedom and courage that has been given them through the gospel of Christ. Their lives, despite adversity (or, especially in relation to it), are to bear witness to the presence and the power of the Spirit (perhaps *spirit* should be capitalized in v. 27) which gives them a mutual and supporting life of faith. Paul's point is easily missed given the translations of the last phrases of v. 27. For example, NRSV reads, "I will know that you are standing firm in one spirit, striving side by side with one mind for the faith of the gospel"; one gets the impression that Paul's confidence was in the performance of the Philippians. But that would be an odd turn given the essentially theological or christological cast of Paul's thinking in the previous verses and, moreover, in general. In fact, the Greek literally says, "I hear about you that you stand in one Spirit, in one life struggling together in the faith of the gospel"—a statement that expresses confidence in the sustaining power of the work of God among the Philippians. Paul's confidence is more "in God and for the Philippians" than simply "in the Philippians." Thus Paul interprets the difficulties faced by the Philippians as opportunities for demonstrating the saving power of God as the Philippians are sustained by God in their suffering.

The Gospel: *Matthew 20:1-16*

A Lesson on Dealing with God

Setting. The fifth major section of Matthew's presentation of the ministry of Jesus (19:2–26:1) portrays Jesus and his disciples on the way to his Passion. In chapters 19–22 Jesus leads his followers along the way as he rebuts his adversaries all the while. Here, we see Jesus acting in an authoritative manner.

In this lesson we encounter a piece of Jesus' teaching that could essentially stand alone. Matthew does not give us a highly focused setting for this parable of the laborers in the vineyard, and for that reason, among others, the parable is baffling. The only firm tie to the present setting in Matthew is the frame around the story created by the inverted phrases, "first will be last, and the last will be first" and "last will be first, and the first will be last," in 19:30 and 20:16. This theme of the reversal of order also occurs in the parable (20:8).

Structure. The lesson opens with a routine, standard beginning (v. 1), which makes a comparison between "the kingdom of heaven" and "a landowner who went out . . . to hire laborers for his vineyard.'' Then in a first scene we follow the vineyard owner as he moves through a series of hirings—early in the morning, and then at nine o'clock, noon, three o'clock, and five o'clock. A second scene occurs when evening comes and the owner gives instructions for paying the workers. The scene develops as the wages are paid and culminates in a confrontation between certain disgruntled laborers and the owner who has the final word. The formulaic line, ''So the last will be first, and the first will be last,'' concludes the lesson.

Significance. Because the parable begins by comparing the kingdom of heaven and the landowner, we suspect initially that this is in some way a story about God. But as we read the story, we wonder what kind of God is lurking in the words of Jesus. The owner of the vineyard deals fairly with one group, paying them exactly what they bargained for after twelve hard, hot hours in the fields; but then he turns around and gives exactly the same pay to those who put in only one cool evening hour's effort. What is just about following the letter of the law with one group and, then, being generous with the latecomers? An average kindergarten child has a better grasp of fairness than the vineyard owner. Moreover, if the owner of the vineyard has anything to do with God, then God must be shortsighted. To those who worked twelve hours and to those who worked one hour, he gives the same pay. With the equal pay scheme, the owner did the most for those who did the least for him, and he did the least for those who did the most for him. And all the logic or rationalization in the world doesn't remove the offense. Commentators prefer to point out that Jesus is not advocating pay scales; he is doing theology not economics. But the logic, economic or theological, escapes us and offends us. In this parable we seem to be looking at both bad business and, at best, peculiar religion. At heart what bothers us most about this parable is the bizarre combination of fairness and generosity, a combination that seems all too unfair. It's the inconsistency that troubles us, and if we are honest, we understand the complaints of the all-day workers better than the actions of the owner.

Notice the protest: We worked all day, but they only put in an hour, and you made them equal to us! These workers want merit pay! Verse 2 tells us that the all-day laborers went to work only after they cut their deal with the owner! They bargained to make sure they would get their due. But notice the last group hired. They never asked about wages. They simply put in their hour of work and lined up to get whatever the vineyard owner gave them. Surprise! Surprise! He gave them more than they could ever have reasonably expected, a full day's wages—the same pay as the top hands. But when the bargainers lined up, despite their great expectations, they got exactly what they had demanded for their wages.

In our little minds we short-circuit God's grace, so that we only get what we bargain for. We live by trying to strike merit-pay bargains with God, and the uncertainty of grace is more than we can take. In a kind of self-righteous insecurity we attempt to control God, to coerce God to give us our due. And in the dealings we make God over in our image, as miserly as we are ourselves. We thwart the richness of God's grace.

This parable tells us good news about a ridiculously generous God, who is different from us. The parable troubles us. It asks us whether we can be freed by the good news of God's generosity to let God be free to love us as we know, through Jesus Christ, that God does love us.

Proper Twenty: The Celebration

The Old Testament lesson's references to manna bring us naturally to a consideration of the Eucharist and to a warrant for the celebration of the Lord's Supper on this day. The nature of the Exodus passage may provide the preacher with an opportunity to discuss the Eucharist (and the other sacraments) in relationship to grace and particularly in terms of what Christian theologians have meant by the expression ''means of grace.'' Too frequently what has been said has been heard as ''measure of grace,'' and so we have perpetuated a notion that the sacraments convey an adequate number of antibodies of grace to ward off precisely so much sin. It is then obviously in our favor to hoard up as much grace as possible against those times when we pick up an unusally large number of sin germs!

The thrust of today's Gospel is a guard against this measured approach to salvation. Grace is available freely from God each day. Those hired at the beginning of the day got themselves into an unnecessary fever because they never considered the character of their employer. They made themselves the best judges of their needs, and so they should have had no quarrel with the one who hired them on the basis of their own estimation of their worth. But when they saw the employer's estimation of the others, then they could not be satisfied with their own. Christian freedom is based on the knowledge that God adequately meets our needs each day. This kind of trust keeps us humble, so that we can never act as though we have grace on account, but it also gives us permission to live freely, trusting the one who has called us to labor in the vineyard. Sacramental grace is not a stockpiling of spiritual armaments; it is an expression of trust in a God who will not fail us in the hour of trial. Martyrs do not receive the grace of martyrdom until they face the fire, the teeth of the lion, the persecution of governments, or the misunderstanding of friends. How unbearable they might be otherwise!

Appropriate hymns for today will include "Guide Me, O Thou Great Jehovah," "O God of Bethel, by Whose Hand," and "Glorious Things of Thee Are Spoken," in relation to the Old Testament lesson.

A reponse to the epistle might be Richard Baxter's great poem, now rarely included in hymnals, but which fits well to a meditative common meter tune such as St. Agnes:

> Lord, it belongs not to my care
> Whether I die or live;
> To love and serve Thee is my share,
> And this Thy grace must give.

If life be long, I will be glad
That I may long obey;
If short, yet why should I be sad
To soar to endless day?

Christ leads me through no darker rooms
Than He went through before;
He that into God's kingdom comes
Must enter by this door.

Come, Lord, when grace has made me meet
Thy blessed face to see;
For, if Thy work on earth be sweet,
What will Thy glory be!

My knowledge of that life is small;
The eye of faith is dim;
But 'tis enough that Christ knows all,
And I shall be with Him.

"Beneath the Cross of Jesus" is an appropriate commentary on the message of today's Gospel.

Proper Twenty-one
Sunday Between September
25 and October 1 Inclusive

Old Testament Texts

Exodus 17:1-7 is the first account of God providing Israel with water from a rock. Psalm 78:1-4, 12-16 is a historical psalm that recounts God's merciful guidance during Israel's wilderness wandering.

The Lesson: *Exodus 17:1-7*

Is the Lord in Our Midst or Not?

Setting. Exodus 17:1-7 is one of the early wilderness stories. The Lord has delivered Israel from Egypt in Exodus 15 and the once enslaved people now have the responsibility of political freedom without the benefit of a country, because the Lord frees Israel into the wilderness. As the lesson makes very clear, this is a mixed blessing, for it means that Israel is still a people at risk. In many ways their enslavement to Egypt has really become an enslavement to God, for just as they could not live without Egyptian favor in Egypt, so now they cannot live without divine favor in the wilderness. Their new enslavement becomes all too clear when the water runs out in the midst of the desert. The crisis simply underscores how this first wilderness generation is a people in training, and Exodus 17:1-7 raises the question of how the people of God will conform to the risks of their new enslavement. In this story Israel tests God with the question: Is God in our midst or not?

Structure. Exodus 17:1-7 separates into three parts. It begins with an itinerary notice (an account of the places to which Israel journeyed in the wilderness) and an initial confrontation between the people and Moses about the lack of water in vv. 1-3. Verses 4-6a shift the focus to a dialogue between Moses and God about the problem of water. The episode ends in vv. 6b-7 with an account of Moses following the directions of God for drawing water from a rock and with a concluding summary.

Significance. Exodus 17:1-7 is one of the murmuring stories. These stories are a series of accounts in Exodus and Numbers in which Israel complains about a threat in the wilderness (lack of water or food, for example). These stories become very negative as we read along in the Pentateuch until finally they become illustrations of Israel's lack of faith in God. For example, Exodus 17:1-7 repeats in Numbers 20 where the drawing of water from the rock of Meribah illustrates the disobedience of both Moses and the people. Even though the murmuring stories evolve into negative stories about Israel, it would be a mistake to read all of them that way, especially some of the early stories like the account of water from the rock in Exodus 17:1-7. The account of Israel at Meribah/Massah in Exodus 17:1-7 is less a story about Israel's lack of faith, than it is about whether God is in fact with the people.

This early murmuring story is constructed around questions. The newly liberated Israelites barely finish their song of celebration in Exodus 15:1-21 before they are confronted with the unknown risks of the wilderness. At this point they lack both place and identity. The early wilderness stories are meant to address the latter problem by probing the question of what salvation now means for the people. Israel's confrontation with Moses in v. 3, "Did we go up from Egypt simply to die?" is such a question. As the story continues it becomes apparent that Moses is of no help in answering this question. He just turns the question over to God in v. 4, "What will I do?" Finally

Israel's question is answered by God, who directs Moses to draw water from a rock. The miraculous drawing of water from the rock makes clear at least two things about the nature of Israel's salvation: First, they were not liberated for death in the wilderness; and second, liberation is transferred dependency from Egypt to God. Given the latter conclusion, namely that salvation is not independence for Israel but transferred dependency, it follows that there is a proper time to test God, and Exodus 17:1-7 provides an illustration of such a time. The story concludes with a narrator naming the location as Meribah and Massah. These are Hebrew words meaning "to engage in dispute with someone" (Meribah) and "to test" (Massah). The RSV translation of the verbal form of Meribah in v. 7 as "because of the faultfinding of . . ." is too negative, and it has been changed in the NRSV to read, "because the Israelites quarreled and tested the LORD."

The issue in this story is not the faith of Israel. Rather it is the reliability of God. Thus the story ends with the central question, "Is the LORD among us or not?" The answer, of course, in the light of the story is yes. Thus Exodus 17:1-7, like the manna story of Exodus 16, is a testing story. Yet the dynamic of testing in the two stories is different. In Exodus 16 God tested Israel with manna to see if they could live by divine grace in the wilderness. In Exodus 17:1-7 Israel tests God to see if the Lord would remain with them in their wilderness journey.

The Response: *Psalm 78:1-4, 12-16*

The Mystery of History

Setting. Psalm 78 is difficult to classify. It is a historical psalm, yet it does not recount salvation as though it were clear and the source of celebration. Rather it is a reflection on the mystery of history. Verses 1-4 underscore how the past is a parable filled with dark sayings. The mystery of history for the psalmist is the fact that Israel constantly rejected God even when salvation was crystal clear. The psalmist tries to provide a perspective on this seemingly paradoxical situation by reflecting on the past.

Structure. An overview of the larger psalm will provide a context for structuring the lectionary reading. Commentators structure the psalm in a number of different ways. The body of the psalm in vv. 12-66 consists of a recounting of salvation history in the pattern of divine deliverance and its rejection by Israel. This large section is framed in vv. 9-11 and vv. 67-72 with reasons why Ephriam was rejected in favor of Judah. Verses 1-8 provide an introduction on how we are to read the psalm (vv. 1-4) and on the pattern of salvation and its rejection (vv. 5-8). The entire psalm can be outlined in the following manner.

    I. Introduction (vv. 1-8)
        A. The mystery of history (vv. 1-4)
        B. The pattern of rejection (vv. 5-8)
        C. The rejection of Ephraim (vv. 9-11)
    II. God's Past Salvation and Israel's Apostasy (vv. 12-66)
    III. Conclusion (vv. 67-72)
        A. The rejection of Ephraim (v. 67)
        B. The election of Zion (vv. 68-72)

The lectionary reading includes half of the introduction, and a taste of the third section, in which God's salvation is contrasted with Israel's apostasy. Verses 12-16 are not a natural division within the body of the psalm. Verses 12-16 recount God's salvific activity in saving Israel from Egypt and in leading them in the wilderness. Verse 17 shifts the focus from God's salvation to Israel's rebellion, which continues through v. 37. Verses 38-39 provide contrast to Israel's rebellion by underscoring the compassionate character of God.

    I. The Mystery of Our Dark History (vv. 1-4)
    II. God's Salvation (vv. 12-16)
    III. Israel's Rebellion (vv. 17-37)
    IV. God's Compassion (vv. 38-39)

Significance. Psalm 78 presents a negative interpretation of the wilderness period that moves in a different direction than Exodus 17:1-7, where Israel's testing is not yet judged to be a rejection of God's salvation. The verses selected from the lectionary text play down Israel's negative role in the psalm by eliminating an evaluation of Israel's dark action and focusing, instead, on the power of God to save Israel. The emphasis of the psalm on human disobedience when the salvation of God is so obvious should provide a telling balance to the story of how Israel tested God at Massah/Meribah.

New Testament Texts

The lesson from Philippians issues a call to put others ahead of ourselves, and it informs us that such a life-style is Christlike and made real by the work of God in our lives. The Gospel text shows us Jesus debating his opponents over what makes one truly acceptable to God.

The Epistle: *Philippians 2:1-13*

The Call and Promise of Christlikeness

Setting. Philippians 2:5-11, the so-called "Christ hymn," was the lesson for the sixth Sunday in Lent (The Liturgy of the Passion), so the following commentary is in part a repetition of that entry. Readers may also refer to the material on setting for last Sunday's epistle lesson for additional information.

Paul spends time early in the body of the letter, 1:12–3:21, exhorting the Philippians to unity. He begins his appeal at 1:27 and continues in a concentrated fashion through 2:18. In the course of that admonition he holds Christ himself up in a formal fashion as the model and source of Christian harmony.

Structure. Paul continues to plead for unity in the verses of this lesson. At 2:1 he begins to mount a christological argument for the harmony to which he is calling the Philippians. Verses 1-5 serve as an introduction for the meditation on Christ in vv. 6-11. After the "Christ

59

hymn," vv. 12-13 complete our lesson by directly applying the meditation on Christ to the lives of the Philippians.

Significance. The opening verses (1-5) are more than a mere preface. These verses call the Philippians to Christlikeness. Christ is understood as the one whose life establishes the shape of the life of the Philippian community. This is a life of selflessness, as becomes clear through vv. 6-11, and it produces an environment of harmony.

It is crucial to recognize the range and force of the theological and christological statements contained in vv. 6-11. Five major thoughts are articulated: First, the remarks about Jesus Christ's being in the form of God is a metaphorical expression of the conviction of his preexistence. With notable exceptions, few interpreters read the line otherwise. The importance of this interpretation should not be missed. Here, in one of the earliest preserved documents of Christianity, is the confession of Christ's preexistence. Often historians assume that belief in preexistence came later in the development of Christian doctrine, but Philippians is testimony to the contrary. Equally remarkable is that Paul, a former Jew, includes and approves such a belief, for there is no evidence that Paul had abandoned Jewish monotheism to make this statement. Second, Christ's earthly existence is declared using the metaphor of slavery. What does it mean to say that Christ took the form of a slave? The metaphor points to his humble obedience to the will of God and to his faithful service to his fellow human beings as he did God's will. Third, we hear of Christ's death. The mention of the cross in connection with the death points to the degree of humiliation Christ suffered in order to be faithful to God and humankind. His service was costly. He did not live to a ripe old age and enjoy the fruits of his happy life of service. Indirectly Paul is telling the Philippians (and us) that the Lord died in order to be obedient and faithful—thus what can disciples expect? Fourth, Christ's exaltation-resurrection is declared. The phrase, "wherefore also God," introduces this element of the confession. Clearly Christ's being raised and his subsequent exalted status are God's work. Notice too that the language ("wherefore") reaches back and relates God's action to Christ's own emptying and self-sacrifice. Fifth, we learn of

Christ's cosmic rule. His self-giving unto death, which issued in God's exalting him, makes him the ruler of the cosmos. The phrases describing the "knees" indicate that all the denizens of heaven, earth, and hell will acknowledge Christ's rule. And the point of that rule is given with the words, "unto the glory of God the Father."

With the meditation of Christ completed, Paul turns directly to the Philippians and unpacks the significance of reflections ("Therefore . . ."). Almost anyone with minimal familiarity with the New Testament is aware of Philippians 2:12, "work out your own salvation with fear and trembling." But very few people know or can deal with the second part of Paul's statement, "for it is God who is at work in you, enabling you both to will and to work for his good pleasure." What a foreign thought to our era—a God who tinkers even with our will! Immediately lights flash and bells ring. Does this mean that we do not have free will? To be frank, Paul would not understand the idea of a totally free human will. Paul understood that humans were creatures and that they were fully subject in every way to their Creator. Yet notice that Paul does not go to the other extreme. He does not cast humans as puppets on strings. Humans are both responsible and subject to God's involvement at every level. This theology and this anthropology are out of keeping with our modern thinking, but they are scriptural, and they should not really shock anyone who is aware of the secular debate over what governs our lives, genes or social conditioning, or both. Paul's point of view is theological, not biological or sociological, but he has no problem with "both."

The Gospel: *Matthew 21:23-32*

Lip Service Versus a Change of Heart

Setting. In Matthew 21:23-27 Jesus is in the Temple precinct where the chief priests and the elders question his authority for teaching. Jesus repels their query with a challenge of his own and ultimately refuses to answer them at all. In vv. 28-32 Jesus offers a parable (upon which the commentary below will focus). He is still at the Temple, and the reader is to understand that the chief priests are still listening to

Jesus and conversing with him since Matthew mentions them again in 21:45-46. The parable of the two sons seems to be aimed at the leaders in Matthew's Gospel, but it can function more broadly when not held strictly to its literary-historical context.

Structure. The verses of the lesson follow closely on the implications of the previous passage and form part of the larger unit from 21:23 through 22:14. The lesson opens, establishing the setting, and then, with a rhetorical question we move to the parable, vv. 28-30. Then, in v. 31, Jesus poses another real question to the leaders (the first was in 21:25), and now, they answer. The remainder of v. 31 and v. 32 are a condemning pronouncement of the leaders by Jesus.

Significance. The parable in its literary context and, most likely, Matthew in his historical context work to expose and condemn the obstinacy of the chief priests and the elders (later the Pharisees come under fire). Clearly Jesus debated with other recognized Jewish leaders during the course of his ministry, and as best as scholars can determine, Matthew's community lived and his Gospel was written in a context where certain early Christians and Jews were in debate and in conflict with one another. But time has altered our circumstances. We (North American Christians) are not Jesus, and we are not a fairly helpless minority confessional community in a hostile religious setting, so this text cannot be replayed with integrity as a polemic against our religious adversaries, even if such persons are no longer Jewish. If anything is the case, we are more nearly like the chief priests and the elders, with our large denominational institutions and secure cultural setting, though such powers over the culture are in rapid decline. It is probably unwise or impossible to attempt to forge a mental identification between persons in the pews and the chief priests and elders in this passage. Perhaps, should one have the opportunity to preach to a college of bishops or to a gathering of clergy, that strategy could (with skillful development) work, but probably not. What are we to do with this text?

Two suggestions: (1) Look at the parable apart from the setting provided in Matthew. Verses 28-31 tell a story that can have more applications than one—as is usually the case with parables.

Jesus declares that what really counts with God is what you do, not what you say. Simply talking the right line is inadequate. In fact, those who merely say the right things are not found to do God's will. On the other hand, what you say doesn't preclude you forever from doing God's will. A genuine change of heart is more than a possibility, Jesus says it actually occurs. To those who have refused God's directions, this parable comes as the good news that real change does take place. The past doesn't determine the future. A bad decision or a hastily spoken word does not eternally set you outside God's good graces. A call refused can be reconsidered.

(2) After the parable proper, the second part of v. 31 makes a strong statement that the Christian community needs to hear on occasion. Jesus reminds us that people who are genuinely unconcerned with God can often be caught up in the fresh movement of the Spirit more easily than persons who are comfortably religious and, therefore, genuinely insensitive to the movement of the Spirit in their midst. Sometimes the wrong kind of religion is more dangerous than no religion at all. Rigid, self-righteous piety can thwart genuine devotion.

Proper Twenty-one: The Celebration

It is interesting to note that the first two lessons today are repetitions from Lent. Then they were used to comment upon the Paschal mystery in some quite specific way: In Exodus we were anticipating the waters of baptism; in Philippians we were examining the mystery of the cross. The reappearance of these lessons can serve to remind us that each Sunday is a remembrance of the Easter proclamation and hence a time to consider once again what it means to be living out the joy of that event all year round.

The use of this Old Testament lesson again allows for the scheduling of baptisms today. Worship planners should notice how frequently the lectionary involves water imagery in a way that can serve as a commentary on the meaning of baptism. Thus the lections, rather than individual whim, might give direction and meaning as to when baptism is to be administered in the congregation. Such planning makes it possible to have more than one baptism at a time and to schedule more conveniently prebaptismal catechesis for those involved. The hymn, "Come, Ye Disconsolate, Where'er Ye Languish," with its image of flowing water, is appropriate for today. The image of "bread of life" is also fitting if the Eucharist is to be celebrated as well.

The epistle has lent itself to two fine metrical paraphrases, either one of which would make a rousing entrance hymn: "All Praise to Thee, for Thou, O King Divine," and "At the Name of Jesus Every Knee Shall Bow." According to one recent survey, the latter hymn has now replaced "O for a Thousand Tongues to Sing" as the favorite among English Methodists! This epistle also suggests the use of the gospel chorus "He Is Lord" as the choral introit for the day. It might first be sung by the choir then picked up by the congregation. Or the same chorus might serve as a response to the epistle, leading into the reading of the Gospel. The same use could be made of the stanza beginning "At the great name of Jesus now" in the evening hymn, "Creator of the Stars of Night."

The Gospel can provide a pattern for the wording of the prayer of confession for today.

Proper Twenty-two
Sunday Between October
2 and 8 Inclusive

Old Testament Texts

Exodus 20:1-20 is the account of the revelation of divine law to Israel that occurred at Mount Sinai. Psalm 19 is a hymn in praise of law.

The Lesson: *Exodus 20:1-4, 7-9, 12-20*

The Gift of Law

Setting. The most prominent event in Israel's wilderness journey is the revelation of law at Mount Sinai. After Israel is led out of Egypt in Exodus 15 their initial wilderness journey is described for 3 chapters (Exodus 16–18). In Exodus 19:1 the journey stops and the reader is informed that Israel arrived at Mount Sinai, where they prepare to meet God. The revelation of God to Israel at Mount Sinai continues for the next 72 chapters (Exodus 19–Numbers 10). In these chapters Israel does not journey, and instead, they sit at the base of the mountain to receive revelation through laws that are meant to direct their worship and their communal life. When the story of Israel's journey to Canaan is resumed in Numbers 10, it only lasts for the remainder of this book, because the wilderness journey gives way again in the Book of Deuteronomy to the recounting of the gift of law, but this time the mountain is named Horeb instead of Sinai. This quick overview underscores how central law is in the larger story of Israel's salvation, and the faith journey that led them from Egypt through the wilderness.

The Decalogue is the first of many legal codes that will be unveiled at Mount Sinai. A detailed interpretation of each of the Ten Commandments is not possible in the limited space of the present commentary, and the reader is advised to use a current commentary on Exodus for a more detailed discussion. The aim of this commentary will be more general—namely, to interpret the central role of law as a divine gift of salvation to Israel. Such a goal is important because frequently Christians are robbed of this gift when they view the law as a burden that was discarded after Christ.

Structure. Exodus 20:1-20 must be read in the larger context of theophany in Exodus 19. The first part of Exodus 19 narrates Israel's arrival at Mount Sinai and their preparation for theophany. In vv. 10-15 Moses is given specific instructions on how Israel was to purify (and thus protect) themselves, for the descent of God in fire that is described in vv. 16-19. The giving of the Decalogue in Exodus 20:1-20 is meant to be read as an extension of the revelation of God to Israel. The text can be outlined in three parts.

    I. Introduction (v. 1)
   II. Law (vv. 2-17)
       A. Who God is (v. 2)
       B. How to worship God (vv. 3-12)
       C. How to live as the people of God (vv. 13-17)
  III. Conclusion (vv. 18-20)

Significance. The introduction in v. 1 is important for interpreting the Decalogue, because it underscores how law is not a human creation to make God manageable, but divine revelation that seeks to transform persons. When read in this way, the Decalogue in Exodus 20:1-20 informs us that law is a divine gift, which is meant to provide insight into God's character.

The body of laws in vv. 2-17 is structured to underscore the point of the introduction. The laws are introduced in v. 2 with a divine self-revelation that is meant to put content into the character of God as savior. The God on Mount Sinai is the power that was behind the Exodus. The remainder of the Decalogue provides a structure whereby Israel can claim the salvific power of God and thus allow this power to descend from the mountaintop, through their worship and ultimately into their communal life. This imagery of a divine descent underscores how worship must be the central channel for claiming God's power, since it is the link between God on the mountaintop and Israel below. Not surprisingly, therefore, worship and how we image God in it are the focuses for the first four laws in vv. 3-12. The divine power of salvation (1) is not transferable to anything else, (2) is not contained in any object, (3) is a power that is potent and dangerous in our world, thus the name of the God of the Exodus should not be used casually, and (4) is available in worship. The final laws make a strong statement that the divine power of salvation must not be restricted to worship but must also transform all communal activity. The final six laws illustrate the point by making reference to (5) honoring parents, (6) not killing, (7), not committing adultery, (8) not stealing, (9) not lying, and (10) not coveting. In summary, the structure of the Decalogue is important for preaching. It does not move from social activity to God, rather it moves from God to social activity, and the key to this latter structure is worship. Worship is where we receive revelation that can be translated into law, which can then restructure our lives.

The conclusion in vv. 18-20 underscores how important it is to interpret the Decalogue as revelation of God's character. The imagery of lightning and thunder in v. 18 is a description of theophany (the appearance of God). The shift back to theophany in v. 18 suggests that the very hearing of the Decalogue in vv. 2-17 was the equivalent of seeing God. This conclusion is reinforced by the motif of the fear of the people, which is a common reaction when God appears to someone. The text is unclear, however, as to whether Israel's fear stems from the theophany of lightning or the revelation of law. The conclusion to be drawn from this is that the two are indistinguishable. Law is a theophany into God's gracious character.

The Response: *Psalm 19*

In Praise of the Law

Setting. Psalm 19 is composed of two apparently distinct psalms. Verses 1-6 are a hymn that praise the power of God in creation. Verses 7-14 shift the focus from nature as a source of revelation to the law. The praise of law as a source of revelation is a fitting complement to the revelation of the Decalogue in Exodus 20:1-20.

Structure. Psalm 19 separates into three or four parts, depending on whether v. 14 stands alone or is included with vv. 11-13. The following outline will divide the psalm between the praise of God's creation in vv. 1-6, the praise of law in vv. 7-10, and a prayer of supplication in vv. 11-14.

I. The Praise of God's Created Order (vv. 1-6)
II. The Praise of Law (vv. 7-10)
   A. The power of the law to transform persons (vv. 7-8)
   B. A summary
      1. Influence of law on persons (v. 9*a*)
      2. The value of law (vv. 9*b*-10)
III. Prayer of Supplication (vv. 11-14)
   A. Request for revelation (vv. 11-13)
   B. Rededication (v. 14)

Significance. The imagery that is associated with the law in vv. 7-10, and the request of the psalmist for revelation in order to understand the law in vv. 11-13, make it clear that law must not be understood in legalistic terms. As was the case with the Decalogue or the praise of God's power over the physical creation, law is understood to be revelation that can actually transform a person. Note how the law is contrasted with different parts of the psalmist's physical body in vv. 7-8. The law that is perfect, sure, right, and pure can transform the psalmist by giving back life, bestowing wisdom, rejuvenating the heart, and enlightening the eyes. The result of the transforming power of the law on the psalmist is stated in v. 9*a*. It results in an enduring fear of God, which is pure. This is the same imagery as Exodus 20:18-20. Verses 9*b*-10 conclude that law is more valuable than gold, because it is able to instill permanent fear in the people of God.

The praise of law in vv. 7-10 prompts the psalmist to request its power in vv. 11-13 and then to rededicate a life of faith to the pursuit of it in v. 14. The law is not clear but requires revelation to be understood. We are far removed from the cut-and-dry world of case law in these verses, and much closer to the setting of the divine revelation on Mount Sinai (Exodus 20:1-20) when God tore into the fabric of the created order through a theophany that called the people to worship.

New Testament Texts

The Epistle to the Philippians urges believers forward in faith and away from the lure of self-righteous contentment. The text from Matthew reminds us of the provisions of God, our own stubbornness and insubordination, and the relentlessness of God in calling us to obedience.

The Epistle: *Philippians 3:4b-14*

Called from Contentment to Suffering and Glory

Setting. In looking at the lessons for the last two weeks we noticed how Paul discussed his situation (he was in jail) in the opening part of the body of the letter, 1:12-26; and then he issued a series of exhortations, 1:27–2:18. In a similar way in 2:19–3:1, Paul discusses his plans for the future, and he issues further directions (warnings and admonitions) in 3:2-21. The verses for this Sunday's lesson come in this second section of pointed prescriptions. Because the lectionary tends to avoid trouble or controversy, the text begins with 3:4*b*. This takes the larger coherent statement in 3:4*b*-14 out of context. The result, upon hearing the lesson, may be disastrous for preaching. In 3:2-4*a* Paul warns the Philippians to be on guard against those who advocate Jewish observances (perhaps the law). Against the claims to authority of those who would advocate Jewish practices in the context of the church, Paul delineates his own credentials. Thus in 3:4*b*-14 Paul is arguing down opponents, not simply presenting his accomplishments. If verses 4*b*-14 are read in isolation from 3:2-4*a*, one runs the danger of perpetuating the serious, distorting misperception of Paul as an arrogant, boastful, egomaniac. Moreover, stopping the lesson after v. 14 rather than v. 16 leaves Paul's statements at the level of himself and never applies them to the life of the congregation, as Paul does in 3:15-16. Unless we are called to preach Paul, we should expand the text. Therefore, the commentary that follows deals with 3:2-16.

Structure. In 3:2-4*a* Paul turns his remarks to the Philippians in a new, even surprising direction—he warns against falling prey to those advocating Jewish practices. In order to show that he understands well the advice he is giving, in vv. 4*b*-6 Paul recites his own Jewish credentials. Then, in vv. 7-11 he explains why he himself turned away from such patterns of piety. Next, in vv. 12-14 Paul qualifies his remarks by telling how his life as a Christian is a dynamic, on-going challenge. Finally, in vv. 15-16, Paul makes an appeal to the Philippians, which he bases on the foregoing statements.

Significance. This is a striking passage, which if read carefully can overturn some of our most precious misunderstandings about early Christian life and faith. First, it is clear that not all early believers agreed on what it meant to be Christian and how believers were to live. Even the earliest Christians had to struggle with the real issues of faith and practice that confront us today. We not only find in scripture the parameters for our lives as believers, but also testimony to the necessity of our struggle to work out our salvation with faithful fear and trembling.

Paul and some other professing believers had sharp differences of opinions. Apparently Paul's opponents attempted to win the day by claiming an authority based upon their Jewish credentials. In response, Paul recites his own qualifications. Many bad sermons, frequently well off the interpretive mark, have been preached on vv. 4-11. Notice that Paul is neither guilty nor disillusioned as he looks back on his life in Judaism; indeed, he was quite content and can refer to his former accomplishments as "gain." But now he is changed, and the gain is "loss" (you don't call getting rid of a bad thing "a loss"). Why? Because of Christ. Paul speaks here from the retrospective outlook of Christian faith. In Christ, by Christ, and because of Christ, Paul's whole outlook and value system was radically altered. Now Paul understands that righteousness is God's work, and it comes to humans as a gift of grace sustained by Christ; righteousness is not a humanly maintained status in relation to God. No, God does the doing of righteousness and humans have it from start to finish as grace. This may prove hard to swallow. Perhaps that is why Paul's opponents are advocating Jewish practices. They cannot believe that they do not somehow need to throw their human weight in with the work of God in Christ for their salvation.

In turn, Paul speaks from his new Christian perspective, talking of the hope instilled by his faith. By virtue of being in Christ and knowing him, Paul is able not only to tolerate suffering, but because he suffers for Christ, he finds his suffering meaningful. Moreover, in Christ he looks beyond the present to the future glory he anticipates because of the Resurrection of Christ. And lest he be misunderstood, Paul declares that he has not yet obtained the glory of the Resurrection in this life. That is for the future; but in the present, in faith, he presses on. If we hear Paul well, we understand that the call to Christ is not an order to be "at ease"; rather, we are called to move on, perhaps in "double time." Paul seems assured of the Philippians' capacity to hear, because he believes that whatever understanding they enjoy comes to them from the work of God among them; and God's work ultimately unites believers, despite the real differences that Paul recognizes and that motivates his words in this text.

The Gospel: *Matthew 21:33-43*

The God Who Gives and Keeps Sending

Setting. The verses of the lesson follow directly on those of last Sunday's text. Readers are asked to refer to the discussion of setting for last week's Gospel lesson.

Structure. The lesson comprises the parable of the wicked tenants, which culminates in a question to the audience (vv. 33-40), the audience's answer to the question (v. 41), and subsequent comments by Jesus to his audience (vv. 42-43). In his final remarks Jesus quotes a passage of scripture and then interprets it by applying it to the audience.

Significance. In the fashion of good storytelling the parable sets up a situation and takes us through a series of increasingly dramatic events. But rather than stating the outcome of the story, Jesus asks the audience to tell him the logical outcome of the tale that he had told. The answer given, a sensible one, allows Jesus to point the condemnation called for by the crowd at the audience itself. In this carefully crafted narrative Matthew portrays the astuteness of Jesus in confronting his opponents with judgment from their own mouths.

As was the case with the lesson for last Sunday, this entire incident, including the parable in its current context, reflects the sharp polemic between both Jesus and his historical adversaries and, most likely, the members of Matthew's congregation and their own Jewish opponents. The lesson does not have to serve a purely polemical purpose, however, and if read from a theological point of view, it can tell us much about God and the meaning of God's work in Jesus Christ. If we notice the allegorical quality of the parable, and if we recognize that the allegorical elements of the story are not merely about first-century Jerusalemites, but also about God and Christ, we may find an angle for reading the text for today. Let us retell this story theologically.

First, God carefully prepared a gratifying and bountiful setting and then entrusted it to human beings. In turn, God maintained relations with the humans, though they consistently refused God's biddings and even rejected God's demands with violence. Yet God did not give up. God continued to send forth authorized representatives despite the opposition and hostility of the humans. Finally, God sent his son with the expectation that humankind would recognize the rightful authority of God in the presence and person of God's son. But now humankind acted most disrespectfully toward God by rejecting and killing the son. From a human point of view we can expect God to respond in kind: to kill rebellious humanity and to make a new start. Yet listen to the strange words of Jesus, "The stone that the builders rejected has become the cornerstone; this was the Lord's doing, and it is amazing in our eyes." God does not simply get reasonable revenge; God's ways are not our ways. Humans may reject God's son, even killing him, but God is not bound by human actions. Indeed, God took the very one rejected by humankind and exalted him in a most amazing way. Humans may block, but God will parry and even advance his causes through the inadmissible human action. As God judges the rejection of the son unacceptable, God acts both to vindicate the son and to extend the riches of his provisions to those who will cooperate with God's purposes.

Told this way, from a theological point of view, the story gets us past the historical origins of the text that can render the text irrelevant for today. Yet if we are ignorant of the time-bound quality of this lesson, we will likely be either baffled about what to do with the text or tempted to lapse into a deplorable attempt to rehabilitate the polemical context of the passage. Thinking first about the human condition or ourselves may cause us to be blind to the gospel in this text, but thinking first and foremost about God will give us an entree into the lesson that yields abundant teaching about God and, in turn, about what it means to be human in relation to the divine.

Proper Twenty-two: The Celebration

If this day is observed in the congregation as World Communion Sunday, it is only reasonable that the liturgy reflect the worldwide,

73

ecumenical character of the event. This effect may be achieved in a number of ways.

The Lima Liturgy is the service used at the Vancouver Assembly of the World Council of Churches and is designed to illustrate liturgically the theological statements of the Faith and Order document, *Baptism, Eucharist and Ministry*. The service could be used in whole or in part to illustrate the intercommunion of those churches that participate in the World Council of Churches. It draws upon the Church's ecumenical liturgical heritage for its content.

With All God's People: The New Ecumenical Prayer Cycle is also a WCC publication that gathers worship resources from around the world. It is designed to be used as a weekly prayer book to assist in intercessions for the global Church, but its individual parts may be used for planning any number of services. Hymnals are also available from the WCC.

The liturgy of the Consultation on Church Union (Church of Christ Uniting) may also be used by two or more congregations who also exchange choirs, pastors, and members for their services on this day.

Begin a search for the worldwide liturgical resources at home. This can begin with examining the hymnal and other worship books to find how many countries are represented by authors, translators, and composers. What members of the congregation speak other languages, so that a lesson or a prayer may be heard in a language other than English?

The rehearsal of the Ten Commandments at the beginning of the communion service has been a long tradition in many English-speaking churches since the sixteenth century. That has disappeared with the introduction of services that are less penitential in character, but the loss of it altogether would be a denial of the gift of the law, which is highlighted in the commentary above. Since the Old Testament lesson is the Decalogue in Proper Twenty-two, an option would be to use it as an act of confession. Following is a more recent form from *The Alternative Service Book, 1980* of the Church of England.

74

Minister: Our Lord Jesus Christ said, "If you love me, keep my commandments"; happy are those who hear the word of God and keep it. Hear then these commandments which God has given to his people, and take them to heart. I am the Lord your God: you shall have no other gods but me. You shall love the Lord your God with all your heart, with all your soul, with all your mind and with all your strength.

All: Amen. Lord, have mercy.

Minister: You shall not make for yourself any idol. God is spirit, and those who worship him must worship in spirit and in truth.

All: Amen. Lord, have mercy.

Minister: You shall not dishonor the name of the Lord your God. You shall worship him with awe and reverence.

All: Amen. Lord, have mercy.

Minister: Remember the Lord's day and keep it holy. Christ is risen from the dead: set your minds on things that are above, not on things that are on the earth.

All: Amen. Lord, have mercy.

Minister: Honor your father and mother. Live as servants of God; honor everyone; love the people of God.

All: Amen. Lord, have mercy.

Minister: You shall not commit murder. Be reconciled to your neighbor; overcome evil with good.

All: Amen. Lord, have mercy.

Minister: You shall not commit adultery. Know that your body is a temple of the Holy Spirit.

All: Amen. Lord, have mercy.

Minister: You shall not steal. Be honest in all that you do and care for those in need.

All: Amen. Lord, have mercy.

Minister: You shall not be a false witness. Let everyone speak the truth.

All: Amen. Lord, have mercy.

Minister: You shall not covet anything which belongs to your neighbor. Remember the words of the Lord Jesus: It is more blessed to give than to receive. Love your neighbor as yourself, for love is the fulfilling of the law.

All: Amen. Lord, have mercy.

This should be followed by a time of silent confession and words of forgiveness.

Proper Twenty-three
Sunday Between October
9 and 15 Inclusive

Old Testament Texts

Exodus 32:1-14 is the story of the golden calf. Psalm 106:6-8, 19-23 is a historical summary that recounts this event in poetic terms.

The Lesson: *Exodus 32:1-14*

The Power of Petition: Part 1

Setting. Last week we noted how the account of Israel at Mount Sinai actually lasted for 72 chapters in the Pentateuch (Exodus 19–Numbers 10). Exodus 19–34 is frequently separated out as a distinct unit within the account of revelation at Mount Sinai, because it presents a self-contained story in three parts: revelation and covenant (Exodus 19–31), the breaking of covenant with the threat of destruction for Israel (Exodus 32–33), and the renewal of covenant (Exodus 34).

Revelation and covenant. Exodus 19:1-8 contains a divine invitation for Israel to become the people of God with the promise that in return God will establish a covenant with them (v. 5). The theophany of God in Exodus 19:16-19 and its extension through the revelation of the Decalogue in Exodus 20:1-20 provide the groundwork for Israel to enter into covenant with God, which they do in Exodus 24:3-8. Everything looks good at this point, and Moses ascends the mountain in Exodus 24:9-18 to receive a written copy of the newly revealed laws, which will also contain detailed plans for a sanctuary.

The breaking of covenant. As the opening verse of the lectionary reading indicates (32:1), the absence of Moses makes Israel nervous, and they begin to think that they need something concrete to assure them of God's presence. Thus they construct a golden calf in Exodus 32:1-6, which creates conflict with the opening laws of the Decalogue. Thus the covenant is broken, and the deal between God and Israel is off. God's response to Moses at this point is straightforward. He will exterminate the Israelites and start over with Moses as a new Abraham. Moses emerges as a central character in this section because he mediates for Israel's life. In Exodus 32:1-14 (the lesson for this Sunday) he argues with God so well that in the end God changes his mind about destroying Israel. In Exodus 33:12-23 (the lesson for next Sunday) he argues with God so convincingly that in the end God decides to write a new covenant with Israel and to travel with them through the wilderness. The next two lessons will explore the power of mediation and in the process provide insight into God's character. Both texts illustrate how the outcome of events in this world are not so determined as we might expect—either for us or for God. The starting over of covenant after the golden calf event, where God was absolute in his desire to destroy Israel, underscores just how much room there is for mediation between ourselves and God.

Covenant renewal. The story of covenant renewal in Exodus 34 illustrates that when it comes to grace God is very flexible indeed.

Structure. The geographical setting of the mountain is very important in determining the structure of Exodus 32:1-14. The story begins at the base of the mountain in vv. 1-6 to describe Israel's fears about the absence of Moses, who is on the summit of the mountain, and to narrate their solution of a golden calf. The action of Israel at the base of the mountain prompts a shift in setting to the summit of the mountain where the focus turns to God and Moses. In vv. 7-10 God tells Moses about the events below and decides angrily to destroy the people. In vv. 11-13 Moses responds to God by trying to dissuade

God. In v. 14 the narrator breaks into the story to confirm the success of Moses' mediation. The text can be outlined as follows.

   I. Israel at the Base of the Mountain (vv. 1-6)
     A. Their fear at the absence of Moses (v. 1)
     B. The construction of the calf (vv. 2-4)
     C. The festival (vv. 5-6)
  II. God and Moses on the Summit of the Mountain (vv. 7-13)
     A. Divine anger and judgment (vv. 7-10)
     B. Mediation of Moses (vv. 11-13)
 III. The Concluding Summary (v. 14)

Significance. The focus of interpretation will be on the exchange between God and Moses in the second part of the story. The central questions are determined by the conclusion in v. 14, which states that God changed his mind about destroying Israel. What did Moses do to bring about such a reversal by God, and what does this tell us on the one hand about human mediation and on the other hand about God's character. A brief interpretation of vv. 7-13 may provide some answers for preaching.

The divine speech to Moses in vv. 7-10 provides the abrupt transition from the base of the mountain to its summit. God's speech to Moses separates into two parts. Verses 7-8 begin with a divine assessment of Israel as being the people of Moses and not the people of God (v. 7), because they are corrupt (NRSV, "acted perversely"). This is the same word that is used to describe the earth at the time of the flood (Genesis 6:11-12), and God's response is the same. He tells Moses in vv. 9-10 that he will destroy them and make a new people out of Moses.

Moses intercedes for Israel in vv. 11-13 by posing two questions to God, which are linked to two requests or petitions. First, Moses raises a question about divine anger in v. 11*b*, but it is really a statement about Israel that reaffirms their status as God's people. Second, Moses raises a question about the Egyptians in v. 12*b*, and their perception of God if Israel is destroyed in the wilderness. The two questions of Moses provide the basis for two requests or, perhaps better, petitions (note the use of the imperatives in v. 12*b*, "turn!" and in v. 13, "remember!"). The first request is for God to change his mind about destruction (v. 12*b*), and the second is a call for God to remember the promise to the ancestors.

The mediation of Moses in vv. 11-13 suggests that there are two criteria upon which we can approach God with the hope of changing God's mind about rightful judgment. It is interesting to note that neither reason for changing God's mind arises from the people of Israel themselves. Instead, the first reason has to do with mission, and the effect that God's abandonment of his people would have on the nations. It matters what the Egyptians think of God, so much so that God is willing to change his plans in the light of it. The second reason has to do with the divine character, which is that God is fundamentally gracious. It is because of this essential quality of God that Moses is able to implore God to remember past promises. And the result is that God is willing to change his mind and opt for grace, even though the situation demands judgment.

Exodus 32:1-14 presents a provocative message for preaching, because it goes against reformation notions of God as being inflexible and severely unchanging. Nothing could be further from the truth. We are no less capable than Moses to change God's mind through prayer, which in turn can change the very course of salvation history.

The Response: *Psalm 106:1-8, 19-23, 47*

A Petition

Setting. Scholars debate the mixed form of Psalm 106, because it includes elements of petition, complaint, praise, and the recounting of history. We will examine the psalm from the perspective of petition, primarily because of the focus on mediation in our interpretation of Exodus 32:1-14.

Structure. Psalm 106 can be separated into four parts. Verses 1-3 are a summons to praise God. Verses 4-5 are a petition for God to remember the psalmist. Verses 6-46 are an extended section of historical illustration concerning God's goodness and Israel's disobedience. Verse 47 is a petition that provides a conclusion to the psalm. (The doxology in v. 48 is best read as marking a conclusion to the fourth book of the psalms, Psalms 90–106.) This overview illustrates how petition in vv. 4-5, 47 frames the central section of historical illustrations in vv. 6-45, and thus offers the perspective from which we are to read the body of the psalm. This insight provides a strong reason for expanding the boundaries of the lectionary text to include at least the petition in vv. 4-5, if not the entire first section of the psalm and v. 47. Psalm 106:1-8, 19-23, 47 can be outlined in the following manner.

I. Summons to Praise (vv. 1-3)
II. An Introductory Petition for God to Remember the Psalmist (vv. 4-5)
III. Historical Illustration of God's Goodness and Israel's Disobedience (vv. 6-8, 19-23)
   A. General introduction (vv. 6-8)
   B. The golden calf (vv. 19-23)
IV. A Concluding Petition for God to Save (v. 47)

Significance. Psalm 106 takes the conclusions from the story of Moses mediating for Israel in Exodus 32:1-14 and fashions them into immediate language of petition. It does this by framing the past account of Moses' mediation during the incident of the golden calf (vv. 19-23) with present petitions in vv. 4-5, 47. In fact, the call for God to remember the psalmist in the here and now (v. 4) is the same language that Moses used in Exodus 32:13, when he also called God to remember the promises to Abraham. The use of this psalm in worship will provide a powerful bridge from reflection on the past account of Moses as a heroic mediator to present participation in petition by the contemporary worshiping community.

New Testament Texts

In the lesson from Philippians Paul makes a series of admonitions and observations that are meant to guide the congregation in living up to the reality of their call. The text from Matthew is a striking and difficult passage that ultimately reminds believers in a pointed fashion that as church members they are not exempt from God's judgment.

The Epistle: *Philippians 4:1-9*

The Joy of Being in Christ

Setting. Much of Paul's letter to the Philippians is practical in nature, offering the congregation helpful advice about their life in Christ (see 1:27–2:18 and 3:2-21). But the verses of the lesson are even more pointedly practical, for here Paul turns from general helpful remarks to specific instruction about particular matters in the life of the church.

Structure. The lesson comprises several seemingly independent snippets of advice. The section takes its point of departure ("Therefore," v. 1) from Paul's admonition in the previous verses (3:14, 21) to press on toward the goal of "the heavenly call of God in Christ Jesus" with full confidence in Jesus Christ, who has "the power . . . to make all things subject to himself." Then, in vv. 2-3 Paul gives directions concerning a dispute between two women, Euodia and Syntyche, who were former fellow workers of Paul. Paul follows these specific instructions with a twice stated command to "Rejoice" (v. 4) and continues with additional items of "spiritual" advice in vv. 5-9.

Significance. It is crucial to recognize the basis of the instructions Paul issues in these verses. The opening word, *therefore,* sets the apostle's directions on the foundation of the preceding words of encouragement in 3:12-21, especially vv. 15-21. The power to accomplish what Paul instructs the Philippians to do is not simply their own efforts and energies; rather they live and work together in the context of the power of the Lord Jesus Christ, who as the Savior will transform the Philippians into his own likeness. Seldom does so much of Paul's deep affection for a congregation come through in his remarks as it does in 4:1. Yet, even this is not mere fondness, but genuine Christian devotion as is clear from Paul's use of the phrase *in the Lord.*

When Paul turns to his former missionary associates, Euodia and Syntyche, he regards them "in the Lord." As he speaks to them, calling for some kind of agreement or reconciliation, we find Paul raising once again the theme of having "the same mind." From the earlier portions of the letter (2:5-11) we know this "same mind in the Lord" is, in fact, the Lord's own mind. Paul cannot think of a Christian or Christians in other than profoundly christological terms. The life we live as believers is completely in and of the Lord. This life is quite personal, but it is far from private. We are held together in Christ. Faith is never merely a matter of personal piety. Notice how Paul feels quite free to call his "loyal companion," another apparently unnamed fellow Christian worker, to involvement in the difficulty faced by Euodia and Syntyche. Although he does not use such language in Philippians, we can see that Paul's understanding of the Church as the Body of Christ assumes a mutuality or coherence for the members of the congregation that makes compassionate intervention and the sharing of difficulties as natural as a hand gently massaging a sore set of muscles.

Verses 4-9 return to a lofty level of reflection and direction. First, in vv. 4-7 Paul describes the activities and characteristics of Christian life: rejoicing, gentleness, lack of anxiety, prayer, thanksgiving, and peace. Notice in these statements the context of such a life: "in the Lord" (v. 4); the motivation of such a life: "the Lord is near" (v. 5); the orientation of such a life: "to God" (v. 6); and the source of such a life: "of God" (v. 7). Far from telling the Philippians, "Don't worry; be happy," Paul directs them to an active life of faith that is anxiety-free because of the presence and power of the Lord. Second, in vv. 8-9 Paul gives a selected catalogue of Christian values—whatever is true, honorable, just, pure, pleasing (most likely, to God), commendable, excellent, praiseworthy. The apostle tells the Philippians that as they give themselves to such values "the God of peace will be with [them]." This remark is not so much a qualification of grace as it is a reminder that there are both edifying and wasteful ways to spend the life God has given us.

The Gospel: *Matthew 22:1-14*

Going to the Party and Wearing the Right Clothes

Setting. The lesson continues to record the teaching of Jesus in the Temple precinct. For a discussion of the setting readers are asked to turn to the materials for Proper Twenty-one. Here, let us notice that Luke has the same basic parable (Luke 14:16-24), but in a different setting—at a banquet in the home of a Pharisee. Scholars regard the setting in Matthew's Gospel as more plausible.

Structure. Luke's version of this parable is much simpler in both content and form. Matthew's edition of the parable of the wedding banquet is highly allegorized (an allegorical ending comes after the parable in Luke's telling of the story), and some interpreters suggest that there are at least two, and perhaps three, different parables that have been conflated in Matthew's narrative.

Whatever the original form of the material(s), as we find this passage in Matthew, we can recognize distinct elements: (1) Verse 1 sets up the parable. (2) Verse 2 is a standard comparative statement introducing the parable-story. (3) Verse 3 and, then, vv. 4-6 tell of sending, invitation, and refusal—simply and then in an elaborate and amplified form. (4) Verse 7 reports the vengeance of the king. (5) Verses 8-10 tell of a new invitation and the work of filling the banquet hall. (6) Verses 11-12 tell of the confrontation between the king and an improperly attired guest. (7) Verse 13 reports the king's condemnation and rejection of the careless guest. And, (8) verse 14 is a pronouncement that comes arguably either from Jesus or the king in the parable, but most likely Jesus (as the punctuation of the NRSV indicates).

Significance. The difficulties for interpreting this passage abound: How can the guests who refused the invitation be unworthy of attending (v. 8) when they are dead (v. 7)? How can the slaves go out into the main streets to invite others (v. 9) when the city has been

partakers together of an evil conscience seem to love one another. They who commit robberies together, who love the hurtful arts of sorceries, and the stage together, who join together in the shout of the chariot race, or the wild-beast fight; these very often love one another; but in these there is no "charity out of a pure heart, and of a good conscience, and of faith unfeigned." The wedding garment is such charity as this. (Augustine, *Sermons on Selected Lessons of the New Testament* [Oxford, 1844], pp. 337-39)

Wesley's hymn "Rejoice, the Lord Is King" will serve nicely as a bridge between the epistle and the Gospel.

Verse 7 of the epistle is the basis for the traditional benediction, "The peace of God which passes all understanding . . . ," and so that benediction would be particularly appropriate today.

Proper Twenty-four
Sunday Between October
16 and 22 Inclusive

Old Testament Texts

Exodus 33:12-23 is an extended petition of Moses for God to accompany Israel on their wilderness travels. Psalm 99 is a song of praise that celebrates the power of God.

The Lesson: *Exodus 33:12-23*

The Power of Petition: Part 2

Setting. See the commentary from last week for an overview of the three-part structure of Exodus 19–34, which is (1) revelation and covenant (Exodus 19–31), (2) the breaking of covenant and threat of destruction (Exodus 32–33), and (3) covenant renewal (Exodus 34). The lectionary lessons for last week (Exodus 32:1-14) and for this week (Exodus 33:12-23) span the middle section that has been described as the breaking of the covenant and threat of destruction (Exodus 32–33). Both texts focus on the mediatory power of Moses. As we saw last week in Exodus 32:1-14 Moses averts destruction by successfully petitioning God to change his mind about destroying Israel. His success does not eliminate his problems, however, because the absence of divine destruction is not the same as the renewal of salvation, and Exodus 33 is a chapter about what it is like for the people of God to be in this ambiguous situation. An examination of the larger context of Exodus 33 will illustrate this point.

The chapter opens with a divine command to Moses in vv. 1-3 to lead Israel to the promised land of Canaan, but at the end of the command we are told that God will not be present. After the sin of the golden calf, God has become very dangerous for Israel, and if he should rejoin them in their journey, he would certainly destroy them. All of a sudden the promised land of Canaan is beginning to look more like swamp land and hardly worth a risky journey through the wilderness. Verses 4-6 describe Israel's mournful reaction to this news, and vv. 7-11 reiterate the point of vv. 1-3 by describing how the Tent of Meeting (the symbol of God's presence with Israel) was moved out of the camp. Exodus 33:1-11 ends on a negative note, because the loss of divine presence is the equivalent of being stuck in the middle of the desert without a map. There is sand as far as the eye can see, with no way out. It is time for Moses to petition God again in Exodus 33:12-23.

Structure. Exodus 33:12-23 goes through three cycles of petitions: in vv. 12-14 Moses requests a road map, then in vv. 15-17 he asks for God to be present with Israel in addition to providing the road map, and finally, in vv. 18-23 he requests a peek at God's glory. The text can be outlined in the following manner.

I. The First Petition (vv. 12-14)
   A. Moses' request: To know God's way (vv.12-13)
   B. God's answer: Promise of rest (v. 14)
II. The Second Petition (vv. 15-17)
   A. Moses' request: To have God present on the journey (vv. 15-16)
   B. God's answer: Promise of the divine name (v. 17)
III. The Third Petition (vv. 18-23)
   A. Moses' request: To see God's glory (v. 18)
   B. God's answer: Promise of theophany (vv. 19-23)

There is also a fourth petition in Exodus 34:8-9 for God to forgive Israel, which will be touched upon in the section on significance.
Significance. Note how the text shifts in the amount of speech that is

attributed to Moses and God. Moses does most of the talking in the first and second petitions until his final petition is just one sentence in v. 18. Conversely, God is reticent at the outset and begins with very little speech, answering the first and second petitions with one sentence in vv. 14 and 17, but then divine speech takes over in vv. 19-23 after the third request of Moses. The form of this narrative carries important meaning about the power of Moses to petition God, for by the end of this exchange, he has persuaded a very distant God to reenter the text with full force in vv. 19-23. How has Moses achieved this goal?

Two motifs are central to the petitions of Moses, and they repeat throughout the exchange. One is the fact that Moses finds favor or grace in the eyes of God. This motif occurs five times in vv. 12, 13 (twice), 16, 17. The other motif is knowledge, which is a result of grace and a prerequisite for living a life of faith; it occurs six times (vv. 12 [twice], 13 [twice], 16, 17).

The interrelation of divine grace and the need to know God provides the logic of Moses' petitions. Two things are noteworthy about this logic. First, the entire sequence of petitions begins with Moses quoting God in v. 12. He reminds God of two realities: that God knows him and that God has been gracious to him. Neither of these realities are the result of anything that Moses has done. Rather they are the result of God commissioning him to lead Israel from Egypt to Canaan. There is something very important here. By beginning with a recounting of God's past acts of salvation, Moses is rooting his petition in the very character of God and not in himself. Thus, once the past gracious character of God toward Moses is established in v. 12, he begins to build on it in v. 13 with the conditional statement, "Now, if I have found favor in your sight. . . ." In other words God's gracious character becomes the presupposition for Moses to request knowledge of God, because this knowledge is necessary for him to fulfill his commission to lead Israel to Canaan.

Second, once Moses has established his dependency on God and God's grace, his petitions become more and more personal, and in the process they elicit new insight into the meaning of grace. Moses begins with the request for a road map ("show me your ways" in v. 13) and then moves to a request for divine presence ("you go with us" in v. 16). These two requests provide the basis for a third petition in v. 18, which will provide new insight into God in v. 19—namely, that God is gracious and merciful. The real effect of this third petition is not evident until Exodus 34:6-9, where Moses presents his fourth and last petition that God forgive Israel and begin anew with them by reestablishing a covenant. God's reply in 34:10 is that he will make a new covenant and perform many more wonders of salvation.

The three petitions of Moses in Exodus 33:12-23, along with his fourth in Exodus 34:8-9, teach us at least two things about mediation that can be stressed in preaching this text. First, that we never petition God on the basis of qualities of our own, but only on the basis of God's grace. When we petition God with this as our starting point we are anchored firmly in faith, because our very petitions arise from the fact that we have previously experienced the salvation of God and know that we cannot live in the present time without it. Thus our act of petitioning is a confession to God that, without grace, we are lost in the desert and have no road map. Second, the mediation of Moses underscores that there is no limit to what we can expect from a gracious God. Moses' immediate problems were solved after his first petition was granted, which resulted in his knowing God's ways, yet he received three more gifts of grace before he finally stopped petitioning God.

The Response: *Psalm 99*

In Praise of Power

Setting. Psalm 99 begins with the phrase, "The Lord is king." A number of psalms begin with this phrase (see for example, Psalms 93, 97) and then proceed to praise the power of God as king. Frequently we observe significant cultic imagery (imagery of the Temple) in these so-called enthronement psalms, which is meant to underscore the power of God. Scholars debate the original liturgical setting of these psalms. Some argue that the psalms were part of a new-year festival, borrowed from the Babylonian *akitu*, in which the creative power of God was celebrated, while others favor a covenant-renewal festival. This debate cannot be addressed in detail here, and the preacher is encouraged to consult one of the larger commentaries on the psalms (for example, H. J. Kraus, *Theology of the Psalms* [Philadelphia: Augsburg-Fortress, 1986]; or Arthur Weiser, *The Psalms* [Philadelphia: Westminster-Knox, 1962]) for more information. In this resource we observe that Psalm 99 is a celebration of "raw" divine power. What is the content of such power?

Structure. Psalm 99 separates into two parts. Verses 1-5 contain praise of the power of God as king in the setting of the Temple. Verses 6-9 leave the setting of the Temple momentarily to provide historical illustration of God's power. The two halves of the psalm separate into three similar parts: each begins by establishing a setting for discussing God's power (the Temple in vv. 1-3 and the three heroes Moses, Aaron, and Samuel in vv. 6-7), followed by a statement concerning the content of God's power (vv. 4 and 8), and each concludes with a call to praise ("Extol the Lord our God . . ." in vv. 5, 9). The psalm can be outlined as follows.

    I. In Praise of Divine Power (vv. 1-5)
       A. The Temple setting (vv. 1-3)
       B. The content of power (v. 4)
       C. A call to praise (v. 5)
    II. An Illustration of Divine Power (vv. 6-9)
       A. The historical setting (vv. 6-7)
       B. The content of power (v. 8)
       C. A call to praise (v. 9)

Significance. Sometimes the psalms that praise God as king are judged as too authoritarian or too concerned with raw power for its own sake. Psalm 99 is certainly about God's power, but we must read it carefully to determine the content and character of power. Verses 1-3 provide a variety of symbols of power. God is a king, enthroned in Zion, fearful to all people and hence universal in power. The imagery here includes symbols from the Temple and many traditional motifs of theophany (trembling of people, enthronement of God, quaking of the earth, and awe).

The symbols lead to a very direct statement in v. 4 about the character of divine royal power. The enthroned God in the Temple is just and righteous, and hence is incapable of overlooking wrongdoing. The second half of the psalm takes the power of God a step further, when Moses, Aaron, and Samuel are all presented as petitioning God in vv. 6-7. God, in turn, is pictured in v. 8 as not only responding to their petitions, but even as forgiving them. When the two parts of the psalm are read together the following insights into divine power emerge, which provide points of contact with Exodus 33:12-23. Because God is inherently just, God cannot ignore evil. Wrongdoers will be punished (v. 8*b*). But when petitioned God is able to forgive (v. 8*a*). This latter insight is what gives rise to the hymn of praise. Verses 5 and 9 are a call to praise, because only God has the raw power to forgive.

New Testament Texts

The lectionary changes books for the epistle lesson, moving to I Thessalonians with its striking eschatological passages, perhaps in anticipation of the forthcoming Advent texts for Year B, so that the years end and begin with a similar emphasis. The text from Matthew simply moves to the next verses in the Gospel.

The Epistle: *I Thessalonians 1:1-10*

Greeting and Praying for a Congregation

Setting. I Thessalonians is likely the earliest preserved Pauline letter, and as such, it is likely the earliest preserved piece of Christian literature. Paul writes from Corinth to address issues and concerns in the life of the Thessalonian congregation. In a nutshell, the members of the church experience persecution by nonbelievers. Exactly what afflictions were experienced by the Thessalonians is not clear, but Paul writes to confirm and direct them in their faith.

Structure. The lesson encompasses two parts of the letter: Verse one is the salutation, which is in three parts—naming the senders, the recipients, and extending a greeting. Then, vv. 2-10 form the thanksgiving-prayer, which itself has identifiable subparts. Verses 2-4 are a prayer report. Verse 5 makes a statement built on vv. 2-4. Verses 6-7 focus on the Thessalonians, and vv. 8-10 remark on the results of the gospel being among the Thessalonians.

Significance. In form the salutation (v. 1) is a standard greeting for a Hellenistic letter. It is both the briefest and least elaborate of all the greetings in Paul's letters. Several items, however, merit notice: (1) The letter is the product, somehow, of coauthorship. (2) The Thessalonians are "church," using a Greek word that described a Greco-Roman political assemblies and that was used in the Septuagint to designate the assembled Israelites in both their desert wanderings and in Temple worship. The word here refers to a local congregation, not the Church universal. (3) The Thessalonian church is located "in God the Father and the Lord Jesus Christ," which qualifies their existence theologically as well as geographically. (4) The titles given to God and Jesus Christ are striking. Naming God as "Father" conjures "creation theology" and evokes the ideas of permanence, intimacy, and dependability; moreover, God as "Father" is a concept out of Jesus' ministry. Furthermore, naming Jesus as "Lord" recognizes his majesty, power, and rule. While the Greek word for *Lord* could mean "sir," it was the manner of referring to Caesars, and it was the Greek word used in the Septuagint to translate the Hebrew name for God, *YHWH*. (5) "Grace and peace," God's work and its results, salute the Thessalonians rather than a mere "Greetings."

All this reminds us that Christianity is not a solo voyage. We are in the life of faith both with other believers and with our Lord. We are called as Church to be located in this world, but we have our existence in the presence and the power of God and Christ. The simple statement of being "in God the Father and the Lord Jesus Christ" is loaded with the full baggage of the creation and redemption motifs of salvation.

The verses of the thanksgiving-prayer hold a wealth of material. In vv. 2-4 Paul and his colleagues give a report of their prayer. We find that as they give thanks to God, they do three things: First, they mention the Thessalonians. Second, they call three things about the Thessalonians to mind—their work of faith, their labor of love, and their steadfastness of hope. Faith, hope, and love—a rather famous Pauline triad—characterize the life of the Thessalonians. Third, v. 4 continues to name what the missionaries do in giving thanks. There is no "For" in Greek as the NRSV and other translations have it. Literally, the line builds off the "we give thanks" of v. 2, saying "knowing (brothers and sisters beloved by God) your election." Part of the thanks given to God is for God's calling the Thessalonians to faith and service. In v. 5 we learn of both the theological origin of the gospel in Thessalonica (from the Holy Spirit) and the true character of Paul and his companions. (The latter matter, the missionaries' character, anticipates a later theme of the letter.) In vv. 6-7 the writers remind the Thessalonians of the origins and character of their faith from a human point of view: They faithfully imitated the apostles, and in turn, they themselves became faithful examples to other believers. Verses 8-10 recognize the striking results of the gospel finding its place among the Thessalonians. There has been a geographical spread of the word and the faith. As the Thessalonians have turned to God and now live waiting for the Son, great things have happened and continue to happen. The Thessalonians are both agents of and powerful testimony to the saving work of God in Jesus Christ.

The Gospel: *Matthew 22:15-22* ·

Seeking the Divine Advantage in Cutting Deals

Setting. Though these verses follow immediately on the verses for last Sunday's lesson (and the verses for the lessons of several previous weeks), they shift the focus of the narrative a bit. Jesus still seems to be in the Temple precinct, but now the Pharisees take up the task of challenging him, which for the moment the Sadducees and the elders apparently have abandoned. From the major previous portions of the

Gospel we are well acquainted with the animosity between Jesus and the Pharisees over the interpretation of the law. The issue here is similar—the lawfulness of paying taxes to Rome.

Structure. The eight brief verses of this lesson tell a dynamic story. Verse 15 informs us of the motives of the Pharisees—namely, to "entrap" Jesus in what he said. The first part of v. 16 tells of the sending of the disciples of the Pharisees to question Jesus, and remarkably we learn that the Herodians are involved in the ploy. The remainder of v. 16 and v. 17 report the question put to Jesus. Verse 18 informs us of Jesus' awareness of the questioners' malevolence and how he confronted them. Then, vv. 19-21 record how Jesus turned the tables on those who would entrap him. Finally, v. 22 reports the reaction of the questioners.

Significance. In writing this account Matthew gives us enough information along the way—the evil purpose behind the question, Jesus' awareness of his examiners' motives, their reaction to Jesus' handling of them—that we can read and make easy sense of the story. The story is clearly about the authority and insight of Jesus. Whatever use we make of this lesson for preaching, if we are to honor Matthew's intention for telling the story, we must develop a sermon that highlights Jesus' authority. The memorable line, "Give therefore to the emperor the things that are the emperor's, and to God the things that are God's" really should not be dragged out of its context and treated as a timeless maxim. It has something of that quality, but its real sense is best grasped in the context of this story.

The trap laid for Jesus was a simple one, but it seems designed to confront him with a no-win situation. If he says it is okay to pay taxes, he will lose face with the masses, who deeply and passionately resent the Roman presence and domination; if he says it is wrong to pay taxes, he will take the side of those revolutionary types, who for political and religious reasons advocated rejection of Roman authority and even rebellion against the empire. But Jesus turns the tables. He does not simply dodge the question and cleverly avoid peril, he actually outwits and exposes both the insincerity and the impiety of his questioners. How?

Here a piece of historical knowledge helps plumb the depths of the story. There were more kinds of coins than one available for use in first-century Judea. There were standard Roman coins, minted with the likeness of the head of the emperor. Some held the inscription, "Tiberius, Caesar, son of the divine Augustus, the high priest"; whereas others read, "Tiberius, Caesar, the majestic son of God, the high priest." Both the image, understood to be a violation of the second commandment prohibiting idols, and the language were offensive to pious Jews. Thus there were other coins available for their use, which allowed them to avoid blasphemy and contamination from the very handling of standard coins. It was a small minority of Jews, however, who were sufficiently principled to worry steadily about the physical aspects. Yet such piety was highly regarded.

When Jesus asked his examiners for a coin—perhaps implying that he didn't have one—they easily and without scruples brought out a Roman coin. The coin itself declared that they were compromised. Already they had yielded to the necessity and convenience of political reality. Thus Jesus tells them if they enjoy the comforts of Rome, they should pay their dues to Rome. At base, Jesus' statement in v. 21 is a pronouncement in two parts, and the second supersedes the first. After all, who establishes the boundaries to which the emperor's claims extend? Who can determine where loyalty to the emperor reaches its limit? Surely only God can do these things, so that God's claims are the ones we humans must acknowledge. If we make compromises that seem less than problematic, we shouldn't haul in God as the backer of some point for our own convenience in the compromise. We all cut deals with our culture, and Jesus doesn't simply condemn us. But Jesus refuses to let us use either piety or Jesus, himself, to gain an advantage in the arrangement. Christ knows us; we don't fool or use him.

Proper Twenty-four: The Celebration

The emphasis on prayer in the epistle suggests that worship planners might spend some time evaluating how the work of prayer is done in the local liturgy.

Prayer has usually been divided into five types: adoration, confession of sin, intercession, petition, and thanksgiving. These can provide a checklist for Sunday to see if the full work of prayer is operating on a regular basis.

Prayers of adoration are those which praise God as much for being as for doing. If we will but overhear ourselves talking to God on Sunday, we may be astonished at how self-centered is much of our praying. We praise God for things done to or for us but rarely for the good that happens to others. The prayer of adoration may occur early in the service as the opening prayer or at the beginning of the pastoral prayer, or it may be in the form of the opening hymn.

Confession of sin is a standard part of most services. More care could influence when it occurs in the service, rather than simply assuming that it always comes after the opening hymn. During the penitential seasons of Advent and Lent, it is certainly appropriate to have the confession come as part of our preparation for worship, possibly even before the opening hymn, so that the hymn becomes a response of praise for the pardon we have heard. Confession may also follow the sermon as a part of the prayers of the people. Indeed, the sermon may be necessary for the people to make an intelligent confession on some Sundays. Confessions of sin should not be too particular, however, as though the worship planners are cataloging all of the shortcomings of the parish. The prayer should be general enough to allow individuals to recollect and make their own confession fit into it. The prayer should also be followed by words of assurance and pardon (absolution), not another prayer for forgiveness by the pastor, as though the congregation's motion for forgiveness needs a second.

Prayers of intercession are prayers for others, and they can usually be divided into prayers for the Church at large, the nation, and the world.

Prayers of petition are prayers for ourselves, the needs of the local church and community.

Prayers of thanksgiving express gratitude for particular acts of God in the world and the life of the church.

Many churches have adapted the custom of dumping all these types (except confession) into something called "Joys and Concerns." The style differs from parish to parish, but certain problems seem to persist. Frequently no prayer is offered at all. Lists are announced, but God is not addressed. Or else the minister then summarizes the list for God, repeating all over again what has been already uttered aloud in the congregation. This calls into question the priesthood of all believers, if the minister must be the one to make it official. Congregations need to be taught to pray rather than to report, and the pastor needs to be helped to oversee the work of prayer, so that the pastor supplements and fills in what has been omitted in the sharing. If no one in the congregation ever gets to the concerns beyond the four walls, then it is the pastor's job to do that.

The whole work of prayer can never be done on any one Sunday, but careful planning can see to a more equitable distribution over a period of weeks. This is necessary if the congregation is to grow in its understanding of its priestly role.

Proper Twenty-five
Sunday Between October
23 and 29 Inclusive

Old Testament Texts

Deuteronomy 34:1-12 is the account of Moses' death on Mount Nebo, his burial by God, and the passing on of his leadership to Joshua. Psalm 90:1-6, 13-17 is a prayer ascribed to Moses. The lectionary does not include v. 13, but it is included here since it introduces the prayer ascribed to Moses.

The Lesson: *Deuteronomy 34:1-12*

Standing Tiptoe on Mount Nebo

Setting. Deuteronomy 34 is the account of Moses' death. The chapter consists of careful geographical location in Moab and includes a reference to Joshua as the successor of Moses, for which the reader has been prepared since Deuteronomy 31. In the present form of Deuteronomy the narrative account of the progression of leadership from Moses to Joshua is interspersed with the Song of Moses in chapter 32 and the Blessing in chapter 33. The account of Moses on Mount Nebo in Deuteronomy 34 follows directly from 34:48-52, where God instructs Moses to ascend the mountain and foretells his immediate death.

Structure. Deuteronomy 34 breaks down into five small sections. Verse 1 establishes the setting of Mount Nebo in the plains of Moab, while vv. 2-4 provide a brief divine travelogue of Canaan to Moses, which concludes with a reiteration of God's promise that Israel will receive this land. Verses 5-8 describe Moses' death and his divine burial, which provides transition to Joshua as the successor of Moses. The text concludes with a summary statement of the unparalleled prophetic role of Moses.

Significance. If we were to classify Deuteronomy 34 according to its genre, it might be best characterized as a death notice. But the point of the text is less about the death of Moses than it is about his vision of the land of Canaan. These are the final verses of Torah, which is the very heart of the Old Testament. The Former and Latter Prophets, Wisdom Literature and Writings must all be read as commentary on the Torah. The final verses of Torah are not primarily about the death of Moses, but about his vision of the land. If the focus of the text were on Moses, then Torah would actually end with a complete cycle that was organized around the career of Moses. His death would bring the story to a conclusion. But this is not the case as Deuteronomy 34:1-12 clearly illustrates. As Moses is preparing to die, the text shifts to a vision of the land just beyond the river. The effect of this shift is that we lose our focus on Moses for a moment and, along with him, look at the land. The introduction of vision in the death story of Moses points the Torah toward the future, which makes it an incomplete story. The result is that our final snapshot of Moses is less about his death, than it is about him standing tiptoe on Mount Nebo, while God singles out some of the high points of the country, before the divine travelogue gives way to a promise: that one day Israel will reach the end of their journey and live in this land. There is powerful material here to be explored in preaching. The central point of the text is that the death of Moses is about the future. The text is a powerful statement how even the very best of us like Moses live by hope in divine promise.

The Response: *Psalm 90:1-6, 13-17*

A Prayer of Moses

Setting. The psalm is attributed to Moses in the heading. Psalm 90:1-6, 13-17 contains a variety of language from expressions of confidence, reflections on human mortality, and petitions.

Structure. The psalm separates into two parts. Verses 1-6 are a meditation on the human condition (vv. 3-6) from the point of view of one who is confident of God's reliability (vv. 1-2). Verses 13-17 introduce strong language of petition, in which the psalmist requests divine forgiveness.

Significance. The central imagery of Psalm 90 is of petitions for forgiveness. In fact the language of v. 13 is a near repetition of Moses' petition to God during the incidents of the golden calf in Exodus 32 and of the rebellion of the people after the report of the spies in Numbers 13–14. Yet, when Psalm 90 is read in conjunction with Deuteronomy 34, it is not Moses' petitions for Israel that come to the foreground, but petitions for himself. Psalm 90 accentuates the other side of why Moses had to ascend Mount Nebo. As we have noted, there certainly is hope in the death story of Moses as he gazes on tiptoe at the promised land, but another reason why the story of Moses ends on Mount Nebo is because he had to settle for visions of Canaan rather than residency after he disobeyed God in the wilderness with regard to the drawing out of water at Meribah (Numbers 20). The petitions of Moses in Psalm 90:13-17 bring to mind his disobedience, but then again, they also introduce hope that is rooted in divine forgiveness.

New Testament Texts

The text from Thessalonians makes a defense of the motives and methods of the ministry of Paul and his companions. While the text is "defensive," it contains many positive statements about the qualities of genuine ministry. The lesson from Matthew presents a pair of texts, the first summarizing the essence of the life of faith and the second summarizing the identity of Jesus as Christ the Lord.

The Epistle: *I Thessalonians 2:1-8*

The Cause and Character of Christian Ministry

Setting. The reader is asked to refer to the general discussion of I Thessalonians which can be found in Proper Twenty-four. Because

Paul and his colleagues give thanks and continue to praise the Thessalonians through the course of the letter, it is difficult to mark the points of transition from one section of this epistle to the other, but after the salutation (1:1) and the thanksgiving prayer (1:2-10) the focus of the remarks shifts, so that we come to the body of the letter, which runs from 2:1–5:11. Thus this week's epistle lesson is the opening section of the letter's body.

Structure. The verses of the lesson are a coherent but developing statement. In vv. 1-4 the apostles recall the origins and the character of their ministry in Thessalonica. Verses 5-8 clarify the character and motivations of the ministry by denying inappropriate behavior and motives (vv. 5-7) and then, explaining how and why the apostles worked as they did.

Significance. Behind the remarks of Paul and his colleagues in these verses lies a peculiar situation in Thessalonica. It may be helpful in understanding this text to turn to Acts 17:1-10 to read about the apostles' seemingly brief work in Thessalonica, which ended with a perilous situation that led the Thessalonian believers to spirit Paul and Silvanus away from the town during the night. With this information as a background, we can infer the problem in Thessalonica that elicited this letter by thinking through the apostles' statements to the circumstances that prompted the remarks. As we noticed in the material for last Sunday's lesson, some of the Thessalonian's "compatriots" (2:14) are persecuting the believers. One of the ploys used by the believers' opponents is to criticize the apostles who fled town by the cover of night. Since the apostles deny certain practices in the verses of our lesson, we may deduce that they are being accused of deceit, impure motives, trickery, and attempting to please humans with a pretext of greed in order to be praised by humans. The apostles dispute these charges both defensively, by denying them, and offensively, by referring to their actual activities and by explaining their true motives.

This lesson is about the true practice and motives of Christian ministry. The argument generated in this passage works from a theological foundation—namely, Christian ministry is done to please.

God. When we work for God we behave in certain ways that do not conform to the manner in which we might work if we were working for humans. To work for God with humans is different from working for people, because those working for God are freed from the necessity or temptation to do whatever it takes to please other persons. Indeed in the apostles' argument they suggest that being in God's employ allowed them to be courageous, selfless, gentle, deeply concerned, energetic, pure, upright, blameless, and encouraging. In these remarks we are given the character of Christian ministry, and in the apostles' use of rich images throughout the text we find precedent and an invitation to preach this passage through image and explanation. A fine sermon on the quality and cause of Christian ministry (for all believers, not merely the clergy—though this text would do well as the text for a sermon to a clergy group) could be developed from this lesson. It could take up the themes, "Christians work for God," "those in God's employ are free," or "freedom is seen in courage, selflessness, gentleness, (and so on)." Each of these ideas could be illustrated with references to individuals or groups whose lives manifest these items in ministry (not merely in everyday life).

The Gospel: *Matthew 22:34-46*

The Christ Who Was More Than Expected

Setting. After a brief absence (22:23-33, see 22:22) the Pharisees appear once again. As they reappear we are told that Jesus is being "tested," whereas before Matthew said they were attempting to "entrap" Jesus. The difference is not crystal clear, though the hostility here seems reduced. Readers may find it helpful to return to the opening paragraphs on the significance of the Gospel lessons for Propers Twenty-one and Twenty-two to remind themselves of the genuine difficulty of using these texts wherein Jesus and the Jewish authorities dispute legal matters. The meaning of these verses is not, however, bound firmly to the literary setting in which Matthew presents them. The concerns addressed in the lesson continued to be vital issues in the life of the Church, so that Jesus' words continued to influence later believers and they hold crucial meaning for us today.

Structure. There are two distinct parts to this lesson, vv. 34-40 and vv. 41-46. In the first section a Pharisee questions Jesus, who gives a straightforward answer. Then in another moment of time, Matthew tells how Jesus questioned the Pharisees, how they answered him, and how he responded to them. Mark and Luke both include versions of these encounters in their Gospels, but in his edition Luke recognizes the distinctness of the two sections and greatly separates the units from one another (see Luke 10:25-28 and 20:41-44). There is no compelling reason for the parts of this passage to be treated together in a sermon (of less than forty minutes!), so the minister may (should!) elect to take either 22:34-40 or 22:41-46 as a text for preaching. In the following consideration of significance the units are treated separately.

Significance. Verses 34-40 tell of the final assault of the Pharisees on Jesus. The Pharisee asks Jesus to identify the most important commandment, apparently in an effort to see whether Jesus could point to the heart of the law that governed Israel's life. But instead of giving a monolithic answer, Jesus gives the first and the second most important commandments. The first commandment is a directive to love God completely and selflessly. Recognizing this as the first commandment establishes the priority of the vertical dimension of the life of faith. We begin our faith with a relationship to God; we do not develop that relationship through other practices. The love of God is the given of the life of faith, its foundation, and its framework! But the life of faith does not end here. The vertical dimension of faith is unreal and meaningless without the necessary complementary horizontal dimension. Love of God is inseparably united with love of neighbor, and indeed the reality of our love for God is expressed concretely in the love that we show and give our neighbors. Jesus comments that "all the law and prophets" depend upon and derive from the love of God and the love of neighbor. Indeed, these two commandments

106

summarize not only the law and the prophets, but also they epitomize the content of the teaching and ministry of Jesus himself. To be his disciple means to live this life of love toward God and neighbor. Verses 41-46 tell of the silencing of the Pharisees by Jesus. Jesus actually riddles the Pharisees into speechlessness. The inability of the Pharisees to answer adequately the question, "Whose son is the Messiah?" and Jesus' demonstration of superior knowledge of scripture serve at least two purposes: First, readers clearly perceive Jesus' authority; and second, they receive a profound christological lesson—the Christ is the Lord! Any reader of this passage should be moved to partial pity for the Pharisees. The riddle Jesus throws their way is genuinely baffling, so that even from the distance of centuries and with the advantage of Christian hindsight finding and following the logic of the question is difficult! The "bottom line" is that the Christ turns out to be more than anyone expected, but the use of Psalm 110:1 (a favorite early Christian text quoted six times and alluded to ten times in the New Testament) introduces a question by Jesus that may well have no answer. The issue raised by this passage is the true identity of Jesus. The Son of David turns out to be the Son of God. A sermon could begin with the difficulty of Jesus' question, asking, "Could you answer Jesus' question?" Then, one might reflect upon the genuine advantage of Christian hindsight and, in turn, move to the christological level of "the Christ who is more than expected." The final theme could be best developed by holding high the two key Matthean titles, Son of David and Son of God. Illustrations from incidents in Matthew's account of Jesus' ministry and also from the forthcoming Passion and Resurrection accounts would be an appropriate way to communicate the understanding of Jesus communicated in the Gospel and articulated in this passage.

Proper Twenty-five: The Celebration

Today's lessons may be helpful in providing the pastor/preacher with a devotional exercise to use in examining one's ministry and its meaning. By the end of October most parish ministers are in the thick of the program year and are busily responding to demands being made upon them from any number of quarters. Is it time to schedule a retreat day for recollection and examination? This may be done in a group, particularly if it is a group that meets on a regular basis to study the lectionary as part of their preparation for preaching. There is an advantage to changing the agenda and using the lectionary as a means of personal formation. But there is also an advantage to experiencing the day alone or with only a spiritual director. Much of the stress that comes to the pastor is the result of being a public person so much of the time, and the temptation is to view oneself in terms of the effect one has on others. We forget who we are as we seek to adjust ourselves to so many demands. It is important to take the time to be reintroduced to the person who once was called to this ministry we are in and find out what God has been doing with him/her.

It is interesting to compare the crossing of the Reed Sea with the crossing of the Jordan. In the first case the waters are divided by Moses stretching out his hand over them. In the second, the priests carry the Ark into the water, which withdraws to receive them. The liturgical tradition has emphasized the first story, giving it pride of place in the Easter vigil, so that it becomes formative for our understanding of baptism. But we may have lost something by our neglect of the Joshua narrative, and that is the value of the cult as a means of continuing to enable and empower sacramental reality for us. With Moses no longer present, the priests do what Moses did, and so contribute to the ongoing salvific work of deliverance into the land. The ancient Latin word for priest, *pontifex,* means "bridgebuilder." The ordained ministers are those who stand as a sign of God's presence, making possible the passage from death to life. In retreat it might be beneficial to ask if we see ourselves as those who faithfully hold the Ark or are we trying to pump the river dry.

Paul, in the epistle lesson, brings home to us what it means to be involved in pastoral ministry with its multifarious demands. He uses an image not incorporated into any ordinals of which I am aware, that of "a nurse tenderly caring for her own children." The nursing with which Paul has to do is the communication of the milk of the gospel. He was "approved by God to be entrusted with the message of the gospel." As the priests made possible the passage from death to life by fidelity to the Ark of the Presence, so Paul, by fidelity to the centrality of the gospel, and not for any other motives, made possible the new life in Christ. In retreat we should examine again our motives for ministry and seek from God that fixed conscience which, as they said of Paul at Thessalonica, can turn the world upside down (Acts 17:6).

The gospel, being two distinct pericopes, has two messages for the preacher on retreat to meditate upon. The first is that succinct job description for all Christian disciples. And the second is that, as the commentary puts it, Jesus is "the Christ who is more than expected." It is this "more" that overflows into our ministry and makes possible a humanly impossible task, makes possible love that we cannot manufacture on our own, makes possible fidelity to the Presence when all around the multitude is struggling to get to the land that has been promised them.

> Lord of the harvest, hear
> Thy needy servants' cry
> Answer our faith's effectual prayer,
> And all our needs supply.
>
> O let us spread thy name,
> Our mission fully prove,
> Thy universal grace proclaim,
> Thine all-redeeming love! (C. Wesley, alt.)

Proper Twenty-six
Sunday Between October 30
and November 5 Inclusive

Old Testament Texts

Joshua 3:7-17 is the story of how Israel entered the promised land of Canaan by crossing the Jordan River on dry ground. Psalm 107:33-43 is both praise and reflection on the salvific power of God.

The Lesson: *Joshua 3:7-17*

Crossing Over the Jordan

Setting. The primary story of the salvation history of Israel separates into three parts. It begins with the liberating experience of escape from Egypt, then it moves to the wilderness stories where Israel is presented as following God on a journey, and it ends with the gift of the promise land. This three-part structure of salvation history can be described as exodus-leading-land (sometimes scholars will also speak of the exodus-conquest model of salvation history).

The triadic structure of salvation history provides important background in two ways for interpreting Joshua 3:7-17. First, it shows how the account of Israel crossing the Jordan River is a transitional text between wilderness leading and land. Second, when we expand our vision of the text, we also see that this is not the first account of Israel crossing water. The first account was the Reed Sea story where the passing through the water was a transition from Egypt to the wilderness, or perhaps better between the Exodus and wilderness leading. When the two accounts of Israel crossing water are woven into the three-part structure of salvation history, it results in the following pattern.

Exodus-(Reed Sea Crossing)—
Wilderness Leading-(Jordan Crossing)—Land

The diagram illustrates how Israel's faith journey with God through the wilderness is framed by salvific events in which God miraculously leads them through water on dry ground.

Structure. Joshua 3:7-17 begins in vv. 7-8 with a divine promise to Joshua that he will be authenticated by God before the people of Israel, which is followed by divine instructions of what Joshua must say to the priests. Verses 9-13 include a series of speeches from Joshua to Israel about the meaning of the crossing of the Jordan. Verses 14-17 conclude the passage by describing the event itself. The text can be outlined in the following manner.

I. Divine Promise to Joshua (vv. 7-8)
   A. Promise of divine presence with Joshua
   B. Joshua is the commander of the priests of the Ark
II. Joshua Interprets the Jordan Crossing for Israel (vv. 9-13)
   A. Meaning of the Jordan crossing
      1. God is present with Israel
      2. God is giving Israel the land
   B. Prediction of the event
III. The Description of the Event (vv. 14-17)

Significance. The motif of crossing through water can be interpreted in two different contexts; first, within Joshua 3:7-17, and second, within the larger story of salvation history.

According to Joshua 3:7-17, Israel must pass through the water. There are no alternative options given, such as bridges or a detour. The experience of passing through the water on dry ground will provide insight into God in two ways. It will confirm for Israel that God is present with them in general (v. 10) and more specifically in their leader Joshua (v. 7). It will also demonstrate that possession of the land of Canaan is God's gift and not something that Israel has earned (v. 10). This point is underscored by the central role of the Ark in the story, which has come to symbolize the saving power of God as a Holy Warrior (see, for example, Numbers 10:35-36). The Ark is what stops the flow of the river (v. 15), and as long as it is in the middle of the Jordan Israel can cross over safely. The point of the story is that what is true for the Jordan will also be true for the Canaanites.

Second, in the larger context of salvation history, the most striking feature of this motif is its placement as a transitional event associated both with Israel's initial experience (exodus) and final realization (land) of salvation. The distribution of the motif of Israel crossing through water underscores how it both begins and ends their faith journey with God through the wilderness. At the very least the framing of the wilderness journey with this motif is a strong statement of how our faith journey is not only started by God (Reed Sea), but must also be completed by God (Jordan River). Such imagery demonstrates how passing through water signifies the salvific power of God and provides an excellent setting for the preacher to reflect on the sacramental power of baptism.

The Response: *Psalm 107:1-7, 33-37*

Praising the Power of God

Setting. Psalm 107 separates into at least two parts. Verses 1-32 are a song of thanksgiving and vv. 33-43 are a mixture of hymnic praise and wisdom sayings. The first section appears to have had a liturgical setting of praise in which a priest would have called a congregation to praise (v. 1) by providing four different situations in which the salvation of God could have been experienced by the worshipers (vv. 4-32). The four situations included those who traveled the desert and experienced the deliverance of God through food and direction (vv. 4-9), those hopelessly lost in prison who experienced the presence of God (vv. 10-16), those who were sick and recovered (vv. 17-22), and, finally, those who traveled the dangerous seas and experienced God's salvation by surviving a storm (vv. 23-32). The second part of the psalm (vv.33-43) appears to be a later supplement to vv. 1-32, which is meant to provide still more occasions of salvation that prompt praise to God.

Structure. The outline of the larger psalm illustrates how vv. 33-42 could be read as a unit, although the lectionary has limited the reading to vv. 33-37. This commentary will include all of vv. 33-43. The reading separates into two parts:

I. A Call to Give Thanks (vv. 1-3) for deliverance in the wilderness (4-7)
II. The Power of God to Reverse Life's Circumstances and to Provide Blessing (vv. 33-37 [38-43])

Significance. Verses 1-7 set the mood of the hymn with a call to give thanks. Verses 33-42 separate into two parts. Verses 33-38 describe the power of God over nature by employing motifs of water. God is able to turn rivers into a desert (vv. 33-34) and deserts into pools of water (v. 35). The effects of God's power over water are sketched out in vv. 36-38: Cities develop where none had previously been possible, land becomes fertile, and the divine blessing flourishes through reproduction. Verses 39-42 focus more on the social implications of God's salvific power. Just as God can reverse desert or fertile ground, so also is God able to reverse social hierarchy and oppression (vv. 39-41), and this reality is worthy of praise (v. 42). (The psalm ends by shifting in genre from a call to give thanks in v. 1 to a call for wise reflection in v. 43.)

New Testament Texts

The lectionary presents an unusual combination with the selected readings from I Thessalonians and Matthew. The following commentary will recognize some problems inherent in these texts and will attempt to illustrate positive uses of the passages for contemporary Christian preaching.

The Epistle: *I Thessalonians 2:9-13*

Finding Confirmation in Suffering as Christians

Setting. Those revising the lectionary show good judgment and wisdom in altering the epistle lesson for this Sunday from I Thessalonians 2:9-13, 17, 20 to the more coherent reading of 2:9-13. The previous lesson was based either on a debatable scholarly hypothesis that 2:14-16 is an interpolation into the original letter, or it implies faintheartedness.,

The lesson simply follows last Sunday's reading. In 2:1-12 the apostles recall their manner of ministry in Thessalonica. In our lesson, 2:9-12 concentrates on the ministry of the apostles; then, the point of view shifts at 2:13 to focus on the Thessalonians and, in the following verses (14-20), their situation in relation to whole of Christian history (at this point in time, relatively brief).

Structure. There are two distinct movements in the verses of the lesson. Verses 9-12 remind the believers in Thessalonica of the activities and the character of the ministry of the apostles among them. Then, v. 13 strikes a different direction, reporting the thanksgiving of the apostles to God for the manner in which the believers in Thessalonica received the word of God. The lesson is a strange combination that does disservice to its parts. Verses 9-12 would be clearer and stronger in combination with 2:1-8 or simply alone; and v. 13 begs to be clustered at least with 2:14-17, and better, with 2:14-20. To assist those who may want to alter the parameters of the lectionary reading, the following commentary deals with all of 2:9-20.

Significance. Verses 9-12 issue a series of exhortations and appeals to the Thessalonian Christians ("You remember. . . . You are witnesses . . . As you know). In treating earlier portions of the letter for Propers Twenty-four and Twenty-five we saw that the remarks of the apostles are made in response to criticisms of their persons and work by those in Thessalonica who opposed, and still oppose, their ministry there. Verses 9-12 extend the effort to call the Thessalonians themselves as witnesses to the noble character of the apostles and their

115

ministry. These verses are rich with metaphors and images that describe the appropriate character of Christian ministry. The Christian in ministry deals with others unselfishly as "brothers and sisters," and forthrightly "like a father with his children," that is urging them to what is best for them.

The next section of I Thessalonians 2 (vv. 13-20) takes a new tack, dealing with the reception of the gospel among the Thessalonians and with the hardships they have faced as a result of their embracing the good news. Many interpreters object to the inclusion of vv. 14-16 in this passage, arguing that it is a later anti-Semitic interpolation into the original letter. (There is no manuscript evidence in support of this theory.) But whether or not someone added these verses to the text (the case for an interpolation grows increasingly weak), the Church has lived with these lines for hundreds of years, and simply skipping over them will neither make them go away nor force us to come to terms with them. Increasing numbers of interpreters see that in terms of theme and language vv. 14-16 cohere with the material in the rest of the letter, and when properly understood they cohere with Paul's thinking in this and other letters.

In brief, in 2:13-20 the apostles remind the Thessalonians of their own conversion. Then they interpret the difficulties faced by the believers in Thessalonica as being in compliance with the earlier experience of persecution suffered by the Judean congregations and ultimately by Jesus Christ himself, and in turn, their suffering accords with the oppression of the apostles. In other words, they do not suffer alone, they are in good company, and the suffering actually confirms the validity of their reception of the gospel. Verses 17-20 view the experience of persecution in cosmic, apocalyptic terms. Satan is named as the power responsible for the persecution of the members of God's Church.

But what can we say about this text today? First, the apostles begin with a conviction that the gospel is "the word of God, which is at work in . . . believers." The good news comes from God, is about God, and finds its transforming force in the lives of believers as God works among them to bring them to receive the good news. Second, as the gospel transforms lives, it reshapes them into uniformity with the very life of Christ. Christ's own life set a standard for faithful, selfless service even to the point of suffering, and all believers in all times and places are called into conformity with Christ's experience. A life of Christian faith is a process of faithful obedience to the will of God that blossoms into the very pattern of the life of Jesus Christ. A secondary concern of this passage takes up the current status of those who oppose the work and the people of God. They live under God's present judgment, experiencing God's displeasure until the end (the Greek behind the end of v. 16 literally reads, "unto [or until] the end," implying wrath now, not necessarily forever as some translations suggest). Third, the faithful life of the Thessalonian church, even in Christlike suffering, moves the apostles longingly to see the believers in Thessalonica face to face. There is a powerful, even mysterious, draw in faithfulness. Superficially it attracts attention and in turn, gives testimony. It also creates a bond between those living faithfully, even when they are separated physically, so that the faithful suffering of some can become the source of glory and joy of others.

The Gospel: *Matthew 23:1-12*

Exaltation Through Humility

Setting. This week's lesson follows last Sunday's text where Jesus completely silenced his longtime adversaries in debates over the law, the Pharisees. Recall that they were hushed by a christological question, not a legal one. The text for this Sunday comes in the context of the exposure of the Pharisees' christological ignorance. Here, Jesus speaks to the crowds in a strange mixture of tones.

Structure. The text falls into two parts, vv. 1-7 and vv. 8-12. The first group of verses focuses on the Pharisees, issuing a reprimand because they do not practice what they preach, but they go out of their way to get the praise of the people. Next, in vv. 9-12 Jesus' words address the crowd, but he seems to be speaking to followers, even members of the Church. He instructs his hearers away from attempts to gain earthly honor and directs them toward a life-style of humility.

Significance. The problem with the Pharisees according to this text

117

is that they don't practice what they preach. Strikingly, Jesus does not condemn the interpretation of the law offered by the Pharisees; rather he says, "Do whatever they teach you and follow it; but do not do as they do, for they do not practice what they teach." What is being condemned? The distance between insight and performance. And this should come as no surprise to any who reflect on the real problems of religion. We humans do struggle as we try to comprehend God's ways and God's will, but still more often than not it is the case that our comprehension, though limited, is far ahead of our action. As believers we may be perplexed by the existence of evil in the world, or we may wonder what in the world we can do in God's name about a host of problems that are so big we cannot begin to correct them. But there are a many matters about which we have sufficient clarity to take action. God has commanded us not to kill, but we go on arming ourselves to the teeth. Christ has told us to love our neighbor as ourselves, but we pay farmers not to grow grain while children starve. Christ has told us that if we have two coats and our brother or sister has none that we are to give one away, but we live in a world where homelessness increases by the day. On basic matters such as the provision of food, shelter, clothing, and the making of peace, we fall dreadfully short of the mark to which Christ has pointed us. Clearly our comprehension outdistances our performance, so that we are all too much like the Pharisees in Matthew's Gospel.

And like the Pharisees to which Jesus refers in this lesson, we fail to do what we know is right as we busy ourselves doing what it takes to gain the admiration of our fellow human beings. We, like they, do our deeds to be seen by others. Ours is a materialistic culture, so we may not take on the symbols of deep religion as the Pharisees did; but we strive with all that we have to achieve the symbols of success that win us the admiration of those around us in an essentially secular culture. Even our modesty tends to be immodest, so we choose the simplicity of elegance rather than the simplicity of charity. The sad truth is that we have met the Pharisees, and they are we.

Jesus' words turn from the Pharisees to the followers directly. We are told not to seek honorific titles. For decades and centuries

Protestants have enjoyed taking a flatly literal sense of these verses and bashing Roman Catholics with them. But there is more here than meets the simple eye. Jesus' message is that we lay aside our efforts and claims to authority and honor because the real authority and the actual honor belong to God. And greatness in God's eyes is in service. Nevertheless, we go on compiling our resumes, and we continue to give and seek honors. We suffer from the delusion that what we can accomplish can one day comfort us. A mere glance at reality should inform us that the lust for fame is as addictive as a narcotic, and the final outcome of being obsessed with fame and glory in this world is an isolated, phony, fifteen-minute existence without room for the gratitude of genuine Christlike service over a long period of time. Jesus' words seek our liberation. They point us away from a consuming concern with ourselves and to the recognition of the glory and honor of God. As we recognize God's glory, expressed to us through Jesus Christ as selfless love, we are liberated from a preoccupation with ourselves and for faithful and gratifying service to God and God's people.

Proper Twenty-six: The Celebration

Although the official observance of National Bible Sunday is yet a month away, today may be the day to anticipate and promote it in preaching. Paul says to the Thessalonians, "When you received the word of God that you heard from us, you accepted it not as a human word but as what it really is, God's word, which is at work in you believers." Paul equates his own human words with the word of God as do some churches liturgically when, after the lesson, the reader declares, "The Word of the Lord."

Today can then be an opportunity to explore with the congregation the meaning of the phrase *Word of God* as it applies to the Bible. The other lessons can provide ample illustrations of how this needs to be done if we are not to succumb to a simpleminded literalism that underestimates the intelligence of the biblical authors. Have we understood what Jesus is saying in the gospel if we repress the use of the word *father?* The Old Testament lesson extended will tell us about

Jael killing Sisera by driving a tent peg through his temple. Is this any way to go about loving one's enemies?Are we to dismiss this as another example of the savagery of primitive societies represented in the Old Testament? Or is this a woman who confronts the threatened evil in a male general by becoming as evil and violent as he apparently was? An old saying in the Middle East suggests, ''If you behave like the beast to kill the beast, then you and the beast are one.'' How does the ''Word of God'' function here?

The preacher will need to discuss how the Incarnation, the word made flesh, is always relative to the cultural setting in which it appears. Jesus is a Jew. We are dealing with what theologians call the scandal of particularity. The word of God uttered in history must speak in the accents of the time, even while transcending time. The Word is more than words; it is the action that affirms faith and witnesses to the divine presence which overcomes our cultural boundaries and limitations. The Pauline word about slavery is limited by the culture, but even within that culture, Paul makes a revolutionary affirmation about the new relationship between master and slave that is accomplished in baptism.

Paul's emphasis is on the word at work in the believers. The word does not stand apart from the community but is perceived in and through the community. Preaching is a communal activity, as preacher and people seek to discern together the Spirit's message to the church. If the word is at work in the believers, then it is not the provenance of the preacher alone but must in some way be the product of dialogue. This then raises the question of how sermon preparation can best be done: in pastoral isolation or in sharing of doubts and affirmations by the congregation with the preacher. The preaching is not finished when the sermon is done. Those who have participated in the earlier discussion may be the most avid listeners, and from their listening there may be a response that will add to the dialogue as the preacher moves on to the next sermon.

The worship committee may wish to work with the pastor in establishing such sermon preparation and response groups for at least a portion of the year.

The hymn, ''Blessed Jesus, at Thy Word,'' would be a fitting opening hymn for today.

All Saints
November 1 or
First Sunday in November

An Apocalyptic Lesson and the Psalm

Revelation 7:9-17 is the description of all the saints singing before the throne of God in Heaven. Psalm 34:1-10, 22 is a psalm of thanksgiving.

The Lesson: *Revelation 7:9-17*

Red Makes White

Setting. The larger context of Revelation 7:9-17 is the opening of the seven seals (Revelation 6:1–8:5), which describe apocalyptic catastrophes that will accompany the close of this age. Revelation 7 is often described as an interlude between the sixth (Revelation 6:12-17) and seventh (Revelation 8:1-5) seals. The chapter separates between a description of the Church being persecuted at the close of the present age (vv. 1-8), and a picture of the Church in heaven in the new age after the saints have passed through the period of persecution (vv. 9-17). These portraits of the Church have been contrasted by past interpreters as the Church militant in the present age and the Church triumphant in the age to come. The lectionary lesson for All Saints Day is the latter half of chapter 7, the picture of the Church triumphant in the age to come, but it cannot be interpreted without an understanding of what it means for the Church to be militant.

Structure. The picture of the Church triumphant separates into a heavenly vision in vv. 9-12 and the interpretation of this vision to John in vv. 13-17. The text can be outlined in the following manner.

I. The Heavenly Vision of John (vv. 9-12)
   A. The Song of the great multitude (vv. 9-10)
      1. Setting (v. 9)
      2. Speech (v. 10)
   B. The Song of the angels (vv. 11-12)
      1. Setting (v. 11)
      2. Speech (v. 12)
II. The Interpretation of the Heavenly Vision (vv. 13-17)
   A. The Elder's question (v. 13)
   B. John's response (v. 14)
   C. The Elder's answer (v. 14-17)
      1. Identification of the Church during persecution in this age (v. 14)
      2. Identification of the Church after persecution in the age to come (vv. 15-17)

The heavenly vision in vv. 9-12 separates into two songs by two different groups. First, all the saints from every nation are described as singing before the throne of the Lamb with two symbols of victory, white robes and palm branches. The song in v. 10 is not about their salvation, but about the greatness of God who is able to save. Second, the angels pick up the song of praise from v. 10 and expand it with a seven-fold ascription of praise in v. 12. The scene shifts from heaven to earth (and presumably from the future to the present) in vv. 13-17 with the exchange between the elder and John. The elder provides the identification of the white-robed singers in two time frames. At the close of the age they were the ones who were persecuted (v. 14), and they now live in the eschatological age (vv. 15-17). The imagery for both parts of this interpretation comes from Isaiah. The imagery of red blood turning white is addressed in Isaiah 1:18, and the eschatological vision is from Isaiah 49:10.

Significance. The larger context of the seven seals as signifiers of tribulations must be kept clearly in mind when interpreting Revelation 7:9-17, for it underscores how the snapshot of the eschatological age is being taken during a time of persecution. Thus the present experience of the Church at the time of John's writing does not support in any way his future vision of it. The power of this text lies precisely in this discontinuity, for it states that our experience in this world cannot be a reliable indicator of the character of God or even of the quality of our salvation. John makes this point through the central image of the text in v. 14, when the elder, who is interpreting the vision to John, makes the paradoxical statement that the robes of the saints have been made white by washing them in red blood. The content of the metaphor is illogical because no amount of experience will support such a conclusion. Red doesn't make white. In the same way, persecution to the point of death cannot be redefined as victory on the basis of literally interpreting the experience itself. Persecution is painful and usually is contained within the limits of human time. Death is final for human existence. No amount of human violence against others can be renamed as redemptive or profitable if evaluated logically in terms of human experience. But the end-time vision is a powerful metaphor (1) because it underscores how temporal human experience is not always reliable, and (2) because our experience does not contain the final word on either God's character or the extent of God's salvation. God can indeed make a robe white by washing it in red. All Saints is a celebration of the same mysterious, sovereign power of God, for in commemorating the dead we are in fact celebrating life. This feast is in many ways an affront to our everyday experience, because in celebrating it, we share in John's end-time vision that is described in Revelation 7:9-17.

The Response: *Psalm 34:1-10, 22*

A Call to Praise

Setting. Psalm 34 is difficult to classify for two reasons. First it incorporates a number of different generic elements, such as a vow to praise, praise, and didactic teaching concerning the goodness of God. Second, the structure of the psalm is determined by its acrostic form. An acrostic psalm occurs when every line begins with a letter of the Hebrew alphabet. The psalm has been chosen for All Saints Sunday because of the reference to the "saints" in v. 9 (NRSV translates the Hebrew "you his holy ones"). The reference to the people of God as saints is unusual in the Old Testament, because this term usually refers to supernatural beings. This is probably the only reference where the people of God are identified as the saints.

Structure. Psalm 34:1-10 is only the first half of Psalm 34. This portion of the psalm and v. 22 can be outlined in the following manner.

    I. Call to Praise (vv. 1-3)
       A. Vow to praise (v. 1)
       B. Praise (vv. 2-3)
    II. Exhortation to Seek God (vv. 4-10)
       A. The Experience of the psalmist (v. 4)
       B. The Exhortation of the psalmist (v. 5-10)
    III. Conclusion (v. 22)

The outline underscores how the psalm moves in two directions. The first part of the psalm focuses on the relationship of the psalmist and God through the vow to praise and the praise itself. The second section of the psalm expands the focus to include the worshipers who are with the psalmist. At this point the psalm takes on a didactic quality as the psalmist encourages the other worshipers to taste God's salvation. Verse 22 concludes the psalm with a promise of redemption to the worshipers.

Significance. Psalm 34:1-10, 22 provides an important complement to Revelation 7:9-17. The good news of Revelation 7:9-17 was that God's salvation is better than anything that we might experience in our everyday lives. The central metaphor used to convey this message was that God can make white from red. Our hermeneutical application for proclamation on All Saints Day was that there is life in death. As we saw this message incorporates a critique of experience. Psalm 34:1-10, 22 moves in a different direction and invites the reader to explore experience. The difference is that the psalm is concerned with the experience of God's salvation. The exploration of salvation is done in the first person in v. 4, when the psalmist recounts an experience of deliverance, and it is repeated in v. 8 when the other worshipers are encouraged to taste and to see that the Lord is good. The two messages of Revelation 7:9-17 and Psalm 34:1-10, 22 are complementary, because it is the maturing of our experience of God's salvation that allows us to evaluate critically our everyday experience with the eyes of faith and to celebrate all the saints.

New Testament Texts

The selection of these New Testament passages for All Saints Day seems related to the mention of purity in both texts. Saints, or sanctified ones, are purified, and they are called to purity (I John 3:3) and blessed for it (Matthew 5:8).

The Epistle: *I John 3:1-3*

Children of God

Setting. The verses of the epistle for All Saints Day are three of five verses, 2:28–3:3, that form a meditation on the theme "children of God." This unit of thought is located in the first major section of this epistle (1:5–3:10), which works with the metaphor of "walking in God's light" to reflect upon the meaning and the manner of living according to God's will.

Structure. The lesson is a series of statements which (1) recognizes the love of God that makes believers into children of God, (2) explains the indifference and animosity of "the world" toward God's children, (3) declares both the present reality and the future hope of being God's children, (4) reminds the children of the promised future revelation of the Son, and (5) calls those who hope in Jesus to Christlike purity.

Significance. The text opens with the words, ''See what love the Father has given us.'' The reference to ''love'' is christological, for the love of God given to humanity was none other than God's Son, Jesus. God's gift of Jesus has had transforming effects on those who believe in the Son, so that they are now called part of God's family. This new identity is but a description of the real transformation of lives through the establishment of a new relationship with God. Yet, as the passage admits, the reality of the relationship does not alter all of life's experiences, for ''the world'' (that is those outside God's family and in opposition to both the Son and God's children) does not recognize the relationship.

Nevertheless, the Elder boldly states the reality of Christian ''childhood'' and goes on to remind the readers that the future holds even more than they are currently experiencing. There is both a realized and a future dimension to the life of faith, and these dimensions are complementary in that the future gives amplified meaning to the present. Moreover, the future hope of the life of faith in the present is not an ambiguous wish; rather, it is the clear expectation of the future revelation of the Son with the attendant belief that his revelation will itself effect the ultimate transformation of believers into complete children of God.

The present status of believers as God's children, their future hope of the revelation of the Son, and their own full and final transformation has real ethical meaning for the present. The new identity and the future hope are a call to a thoroughly Christlike existence in the present. Purity of life (or sanctity) is the proper preparation for full childhood, for believers are called now to be as they will be when the Son is revealed. In this thinking, Christian hope is not pie-in-the-sky; rather, it is the substance and motivation of real life in the present world. A sermon or meditation on this lesson should deal with the God-givenness of ''childhood,'' the christological basis of our new identity, the continuity between current Christian living and the future expectation of the realization of God redemption.

The Gospel: *Matthew 5:1-12*

The Blessings of Discipleship

Setting. Matthew 5:1-12 is the lesson for the Fourth Sunday After the Epiphany in Year A, so the following commentary is essentially a repetition of that entry.

In Matthew 4:24-25 one learns that Jesus attracts a large following as he goes about his ministry. This week's text opens with Jesus looking upon that following and, in turn, teaching them about the characteristics of his disciples. Verses 1-12 are formally the beginning of the famous section of Matthew's Gospel called "The Sermon on the Mount" (Matthew 5:1–7:28). The lectionary reading offers direction for knowing what it means to be a follower of Jesus Christ.

Structure. Verses 1-2 introduce the well-known "Beatitudes" in vv. 3-12. The material is structured deliberately, as can be seen from a careful comparison of this passage with the comparable text in Luke 6:20-23. There are four pronouncements common to the two Gospels, and Matthew's list contains five beatitudes without parallel in Luke. Luke's text seems more primitive than Matthew's balanced and elaborate passage. Matthew offers two sets of sayings structured in an A/B/A/B pattern, which cohere by beginning and ending with the line "for theirs is the kingdom of heaven," and both end with a stated concern for "righteousness":

A   poor in spirit, for theirs is the kingdom of heaven
B   mourn
A   meek
B   hunger and thirst for righteousness
Á   merciful
Ḃ   pure in heart
Á   peacemakers
Ḃ   persecuted for righteousness, for theirs is the kingdom of heaven

The final beatitude, which is somewhat different in form and tone, epitomizes the beatitude for the persecuted.

Significance. Matthew tells the reader that Jesus "went up on the mountain." He does not name the mountain, however, for it is of more symbolic than geographical importance. In the Old Testament mountains are regularly the place where divine revelation occurs. One thinks immediately of Horeb, Sinai, and Zion. A precise identification is not necessary, but the Beatitudes begin the Sermon in a manner similar to the way the Ten Commandments introduce the law, so that the analogy to Matthew's mountain may well be Sinai, with Jesus re-presenting the law as the "New Moses." Nevertheless, on a place where one expects a divine communication, Jesus sits (the normal, authoritative teaching posture of his time) and then, speaks.

Even the basic pertinent information for interpretation of the Beatitudes is voluminous, so the following remarks focus on matters to stimulate thoughts for preaching.

First, throughout the Beatitudes, Jesus' address is to "you" in the plural Greek form. These statements relate to community life, not merely personal piety. Jesus' words describe the life that believers are to live in relation to one another and to the world.

Second, in v. 3 Matthew "spiritualized" the concept of the poor (as he does mourning, hunger, and thirst in the subsequent lines), moving beyond a literal sense. In Israel, a class of people, often genuinely impoverished, called themselves "the poor." The term designated a style of piety that allowed nothing other than God to be the basis of security. Being poor, having nothing, was celebrated as an opportunity for absolute, radical dependence upon God. Such piety was not passive, however, for faith was no placebo. Persons fully committed to God were extremely free. One thinks of John the Baptist and Jesus as examples of such piety.

Third, from the statement in v. 4 itself, it is not immediately clear how Matthew interpreted mourning as a spiritual disposition. The parallel line in v. 6 mentions righteousness as the object of hunger and thirst, so that perhaps those mourning are grieved by their lack of righteousness. In any case, the promise to the mourners is striking:

They shall be comforted. This line contains a common phenomenon in biblical literature—namely, the "divine passive." The unnamed actor in such a text is God. The use of the passive came originally through the concern of pious Jews to avoid using God's name or even referring to God directly. Verse 6 is quite similar to this line, though its sense is more straightforward.

Fourth, the reference to the meek in v. 5 recalls Psalm 37:11. "Meekness" is akin to "poverty" in much of the Old Testament, and as such it refers to the submission of human will to the divine.

Fifth, v. 7 foreshadows the words of the Lord's Prayer, "Forgive us our debts, as we forgive our debtors." The NRSV translation, "for they shall receive mercy," may be misleading. This does not mean that we gain mercy by being merciful; rather, grace begets grace. Those experiencing divine mercy live merciful lives that bespeak the mercy which they themselves receive.

Sixth, the reference in v. 8 to "the pure in heart" indicates persons who are singlemindedly devoted to God. Thus the promise "they shall see God." Søren Kierkegaard wrote eloquently of this notion in *Purity of Heart*, as did Jonathan Edwards in *True Virtue*. This line is a positive critique of divided loyalties that compromise complete devotion to God.

Seventh, in v. 9 the "peacemakers" refer to persons who are actively engaged in the pursuit of peace. Clearly they are doing God's will, as though they were, and in fact are, God's own children.

Eighth, v. 10 blesses those "persecuted for righteousness' sake" and promises them "the kingdom of heaven." This statement is consistent with all that went before, but the pronouncement alters the tone of the passage as it introduces the idea of experiencing persecution as a Christian. This frank recognition that true piety does not guarantee an increased popularity is a sobering reminder that Christian faith is not a rosy-glowing, saccharin-sweet piety. True faith, Jesus says, may be tough and costly. The more elaborate statement in vv. 11-12 develops this idea and forms a crucial parallel between suffering for righteousness' sake and suffering for Jesus' sake.

All Saints: The Celebration

All Saints Day is the Church's Memorial Day, a time to remember those who have died in the faith of Christ. It is traditionally celebrated on November 1, but may be observed on the first Sunday in November instead. For Protestants, for whom the observance of special days for saints may be problematic, we understand that in the strict sense of the word this is a festival day in honor of the grace of Christ. In the classical tradition the calendar was divided into two patterns, the dominical cycle and the sanctoral cycle. The dominical cycle included all Sundays and other days of the year which celebrated and recalled the major events in the life of our Lord (hence "dominical"). The sanctoral cycle emerged as the Church sought to remember the witness of particular saints, especially martyrs, on the day of their death (their heavenly birthday). Gradually, however, the popularity of saints days tended to crowd out the days of the dominical cycle as the number of saints to be remembered grew. By the time of the Reformation only the most major of the days in the dominical cycle were not displaced by one of the saints, and so the reaction was to get rid of saints days altogether. Four hundred years later there is a growing appreciation of the witness of the saints and the appropriateness of remembering them on certain days. Many denominational calendars have now restored saints to the list, including very recent ones such as Martin Luther King, Jr., Dietrich Bonhoeffer, and Florence Nightingale. All Saints Day, however, is not a part of the sanctoral cycle. It is part of the dominical cycle (hence it can be transferred to the following Lord's Day), because in the last analysis it is not a celebration (or deification) of the saints but rather of the victory of the grace of Christ in the saints. We are celebrating what Christ has done in and through the witness of us, the saints, through the ages.

The color white is appropriate for today, as is the celebration of Holy Communion. This can also be an opportunity to explore in the sermon the meaning of the creedal term "the communion of saints" in relation to the words of the eucharistic preface, "with . . . all the company of heaven we praise your name. . . ." The names of those who have died since the previous All Saints service may be read and remembered as part of the service.

The administration of Holy Baptism is particularly appropriate for today, since in baptism we make new saints, in keeping with the New Testament's understanding of the word. As we remember those saints who have gone before, so we also rejoice in God's provision that the gospel will not be left without witness as others are added to the apostolic company.

See Hickman, et al., *New Handbook of the Christian Year (1992)* for expanded suggestions for a full service for this day.

Proper Twenty-seven
Sunday Between November 6 and 12 Inclusive

Old Testament Texts

Joshua 24 recounts Israel's covenant renewal with God at Shechem. Psalm 78 is a wisdom psalm that teaches by recounting history.

The Lesson: *Joshua 24:1-3a, 14-25*

Covenant Renewal at Shechem

Setting. The book of Joshua is about Israel's conquest of Canaan, and as such, it can be read as the completion of the story of salvation. The recounting of Israel's salvation history in vv. 4-13 (the section that has been eliminated in the lectionary reading) provides the outline of the story of salvation. God called the ancestors out of a larger cultural setting to be the people of God (vv. 3-4), God rescued Israel from slavery in Egypt (vv. 5-7*a*), led them through the wilderness (vv. 7*b*-10), and finally gave them the land of Canaan through holy war (vv. 11-13). The covenant ceremony at Shechem in Joshua 24 provides a conclusion to salvation history by formalizing the obligations and relationships between God and Israel to ensure that the people of God flourish in their new found life in the land.

Structure. Joshua 24:1-3*a*, 14-25 separates into five sections. Verse 1 establishes the setting (Shechem) and the participants in the ritual (elders, judges, officers, God), before Joshua addresses the people with divine speech in vv. 2-3*a*, "Thus says the Lord . . ." at which time God recounts salvation history. There is a shift from past actions of God (vv. 2-13) to the present moment in vv. 14-21, when Joshua addresses the people ("Now therefore revere the Lord . . .") and confronts them with the choice of serving God. Verses 22-24 confirm Israel's choice with the legal language of witnessing. Finally, v. 25 provides a concluding commentary by labeling this entire process as a covenant.

Significance. Joshua 24 is about choice. The entire text is a formal ritual or dialogue between Joshua (representing God) and Israel about choice, which carries legal overtones. God has delivered on the promise of salvation and Israel is being forced to decide whether or not to follow God. The choice is anything but casual, and this is underscored both in the structure of the text and in the language of the discourse. Note that after God's past acts of salvation have been reviewed in vv. 2-13, and the text moves into the present time in vv. 14-21 for the purpose of confronting Israel with the need to make a decision to follow God, that the process of confrontation is repeated. The first cycle includes vv. 14-18. Here Joshua presents Israel with the choice of serving God (vv. 14-15), to which Israel readily responds in the affirmative (vv. 16-18). But it is as though Israel's decision is too casual for Joshua, because a whole new cycle begins again in vv. 19-21, with Joshua confronting Israel with the need and danger of making a choice to enter into covenant with God (vv. 19-20), to which the people respond again by expressing their wish to follow God (v. 21). The language of Joshua's second speech is meant to explain why the whole process is repeated. He tells Israel that they cannot serve God, because God is separate (holy) from them, and that a choice in favor of following God could be very dangerous for them, because God could do them harm if they failed to live up to their obligations.

The central point in preaching Joshua 24 is that for all the promise and hope that comes with God's salvation, it also carries with it a dangerous aspect in the form of accountability and obligations. Choosing to enter into covenant with God, and hence to become part of the people of God, is not like buying a new car. An impulsive decision here may mean a few years of disappointment or perhaps a loss of money in an earlier-than-expected exchange. The point of Joshua 24 is that God does not tolerate exchanges on the part of the people of God. Covenant with God is an unending commitment, not to be entered into lightly.

The Response: *Psalm 78:1-7*

The Mystery of History

Setting. Psalm 78 is difficult to classify. It is a historical psalm, yet is does not recount salvation as though it were clear and the source of celebration. Rather it is a reflection on the mystery of history. Verses 1-4 underscore how the past is a parable filled with dark sayings. The mystery of history for the psalmist is the fact that Israel constantly rejected God even when salvation was crystal clear. The psalmist tries to provide a perspective on this seemingly paradoxical situation by reflecting on the past.

Structure. An overview of the larger psalm will provide a context for structuring the lectionary reading. Commentators structure the psalm in a number of different ways. The body of the psalm in vv. 12-66 consists of a recounting of salvation history in the pattern of divine deliverance and its rejection by Israel. This large section is framed in vv. 9-11 and vv. 67-72 with reasons why Ephraim was rejected in favor of Judah. Verses 1-8 provide an introduction on how we are to read the psalm (vv. 1-4) and on the pattern of salvation and its rejection (vv. 5-8). The entire psalm can be outlined in the following manner.

   I. Introduction (vv. 1-11)
      A. The mystery of history (vv. 1-4)
      B. The pattern of rejection (vv. 5-8)
      C. The rejection of Ephraim (vv. 9-11)
   II. God's Past Salvation and Israel's Apostasy (vv. 12-66)
 III. Conclusion (vv. 67-72)
      A. The rejection of Ephraim (v. 67)
      B. The election of Zion (vv. 68-72)

Significance. The lectionary reading is taken entirely from the opening section. When it is read with Joshua 24, the emphasis on passing along the story of God's past acts of salvation to the next generation (vv. 5-6) takes on an ominous overtone. Choosing for God is dangerous and the account of Ephraim in the larger context of the psalm illustrates this point. Verse 7, however, moves in the other direction by emphasizing how such a choice is also the only way for hope to flourish. By having the psalm end at v. 7, with its emphasis on hope, it provides a positive counter voice to the Old Testament lesson. Covenant with God may be dangerous, but the danger is certainly worth the risk.

New Testament Texts

Both lessons are drawn from the explicitly eschatological portions of the New Testament. Both passages treat the theme of the so-called second coming of Christ, and in different ways both passages are concerned with the implications of Christ's coming for everyday Christian living.

The Epistle: *I Thessalonians 4:13-18*

Encourage One Another with These Words

Setting. Having greeted the Thessalonians (see Proper Twenty-four), having defended the character of their ministry (see Proper Twenty-five), and having addressed the suffering that the Thessalonians are experiencing (see Proper Twenty-six), the apostles explained why they wrote to the church (chapter 3). Then, in chapter 4 the apostles instruct the Thessalonians on a series of broad topics: living a decent life (vv. 1-8); Christian love (vv. 9-12); and, in turn, in the verses of this week's lesson, death and Christian assurance. The teaching in 4:13-18 is thoroughly eschatological.

Structure. There are four related movements in this passage. Verse 13 announces the topic, "those who have died"; and it recognizes the motivation for the following teaching: "so that you may not grieve as others who have no hope.'' Verse 14 then sets out the christological foundation of the position that the apostles propound and here explain: ''God will bring with [Jesus] those who have died.'' Verses 15-17 describe the events at the coming of Christ using the images of apocalyptic eschatology. Finally, v. 18 applies the teaching about the coming and the fate of the dead and the living to the lives of the Thessalonians.

Significance. The apostles address those with painful questions about the destiny of other believers who have died prior to the coming of Christ. The eschatological teaching in this passage is offered pastorally as a word of assurance rather than didactically as sheer doctrine. Yet this pastoral word is based on and contains traditional beliefs, so that it is not simply consolation but consolation with doctrinal substance.

It is crucial to notice that the foundation of the vision of the end laid out before the Thessalonians is the conviction that as Christ died and was raised and is coming, so the fate of those who believe in him is bound up with the reality of his own activity. The dead are dead in Christ, and as he lives they will live. Moreover, as he will come in power to execute God's judgment, the lives of those who have died in him are reconstituted, or better, re-created by that same godly power. For those who work with this text for instructing and forming genuine Christian consciousness, it is important to recognize that the dead in Christ are raised as Christ was, but they are not merely resuscitated. As life comes to us in the first place as a gift from God, new life comes to us afresh as another gift from God. In Christian thought we do not have souls that are trapped in our bodies and waiting to be released at death. Instead, we are souls, and at death our creaturely existence ceases. The good news of the gospel is that God does not allow death to destroy the creatures whom God made and loves; rather, God acts in Christ to give us new life, not so much preserving us as re-creating us.

It is easy to be distracted or to become lost in the bold apocalyptic images of this text. But to do so is to miss the real point and force of this passage. Having laid a christological foundation for the teaching, the metaphors of apocalyptic eschatology tell us of an event that comes from beyond the boundaries of daily life. The images of this text point us to divine power that comes from beyond us but has profound meaning for and effect upon our lives. Christ's coming is God's work, and it is extraordinary. Whatever we attempt to make of these striking images, we must resist the rational urge to domesticate the passage by explaining it away. The power of the passage is in its testimony to the power of God, which has grasped our lives through faith and which has the capacity to hold us firmly, even in defiance of death.

Finally, we must notice v. 18. Here the apostles show the relevance and the purpose of eschatology in Christian life. Having taught the Thessalonians about the end, the apostles direct them, "Therefore encourage one another with these words." Far from being esoteric speculation, Christian eschatology directs us into edifying action in relation to others in the context of daily life. Eschatology motivates ethics. We do not merely have and hold the teaching about the future and the fate of the dead, rather that teaching is given to us so that we will minister to one another. Because we are told of Christ's coming, we are given hope that frees us to care for others.

The Gospel: *Matthew 25:1-13*

The Necessity of Being Prepared

Setting. Each of the Synoptic Gospels completes the recounting of the ministry of Jesus with sections of teaching material that are referred to as "little apocalypses"—that is, the last words of Jesus prior to the Passion narrative are remembered as his teachings about the future. In arranging the material in this fashion, Matthew (along with Mark and Luke) shows the concern of the early Church to connect the time after Easter firmly with the time of the historical ministry of Jesus. The early Church understood that its time was not separated from the time of Jesus, indeed in his teaching he pointed forward to their time and, thereby, made it his and theirs. Matthew offers the greatest volume of such teaching about the future. Among the items that are unique to his Gospel are the verses of this Sunday's lesson.

Structure. The parable of the ten bridesmaids (or virgins) presents us with a striking array of images and events. There are basically three scenes. 1) Two elements set up the story: Verses 1-4 tell of the ten bridesmaids and distinguish and divide them evenly as either foolish or wise. Then, v. 5 reports both that the bridegroom has been delayed and that all the bridesmaids fell asleep. 2) With this situation established, v. 6 shifts the circumstances. The bridegroom is sighted and the bridesmaids are called to meet him. Next, in vv. 7-10 we learn that this call produces a crisis for the foolish who have to leave to purchase needed oil, and while they are gone the wise enter the wedding banquet with the bridegroom and the door is shut. 3) The final scene occurs when, in v. 11, the foolish return and call for admission, but in v. 12 the bridegroom refuses them. After this story comes a summarizing tagline (v. 13) that fits oddly with the foregoing story.

Significance. This parable is a thorough allegory of the second coming of Christ. The bridesmaids represent the Church as Matthew knows it with its mixed congregation. The bridegroom is the coming Christ, and his delay is the wait the Church experiences in anticipation of his arrival. Oddly, in this story all fall asleep, and while the charge to "keep awake" comes in v. 13, in the parable neither the wise nor the foolish are condemned for their sleeping. Rather, the issue that separates them in the parable is the adequacy of their preparation. The arrival of the bridegroom represents, of course, the parousia; and the admission of the wise to the banquet and the exclusion of the foolish point to the promise of discriminating judgment at the coming of Christ.

The point of this allegory is clear: During the indefinite period prior to the coming of Christ the members of the Church are required to be prepared at all times for his promised arrival. This parable is not, however, a mere moral lesson that calls for Christians to "be good." Sermons frequently treat the text in this way, but they tend to miss the purpose of preparedness. We are not prepared by doing the right things simply so that we can get into the wedding banquet; rather the point of our preparation is so that we will be ready to participate in the joy of the banquet. We are told in this parable that prior to the coming of Christ we are to attend to tasks that anticipate the arrival of the bridegroom and the commencement of the banquet. We do not do "A" in order to get "B." Instead, here and now we are about the things of the banquet itself. Our anticipation of the coming of Christ means that our expectation of the full advent of the kingdom of heaven allows the substance of the kingdom itself to grasp our lives and to shape us into citizens practiced in the life-style of the kingdom of our Lord. The lamps of the bridesmaids became the lights by which the dancers at the wedding banquet performed. Our preparation is more than an admission ticket, it is our training for attendance.

As we encounter eschatological texts such as this we must labor to eliminate the stark distance, which is implied by the passages themselves, between our present and God's future. We do not do this by simply hauling the promises of the future into the present, thus producing an overly realized eschatology. Instead, we must allow the promise of the future to call us forth in the present. God's future draws us and directs us as we live in the present, anticipating what God's power will do in and through the coming of our Lord Jesus Christ. God's future claims the present, for indeed Christ is not only coming, he has already come. Those in church don't need to hear the threatening dimensions—it will create an us/them split—but without a doubt, Jesus thought God had standards and that humans ought to take them very seriously for their true good.

Proper Twenty-seven: The Celebration

Today's epistle and Gospel begin to concentrate in a particular way on the eschatological element of the gospel as we move towards the end of the Christian year. The First Sunday in Advent will serve as a climax to this series of lessons, thus making the point that the Christian year is more spiral than cycle.

For those who wish to observe this day as All Saints Sunday, then the propers for All Saints should be used rather than trying to impose that theme upon these lessons. The only point where a sharing of

lessons might be possible is to use Proper Twenty-seven's Old
Testament lesson in Joshua 24 as an example of an entire community
declaring its allegiance and reliance upon the Lord. This would seem to
call for the use of "God Moves in a Mysterious Way," with its stanza

> Ye fearful saints, fresh courage take;
> The clouds ye so much dread
> Are big with mercy, and shall break
> In blessings on your head.

For these remaining Sundays in the year the conclusion of
I Thessalonians, which does not appear in the lectionary, may serve
appropriately as a benediction: "May the God of peace himself
sanctify you entirely; and may your spirit and soul and body be kept
sound and blameless at the coming of our Lord Jesus Christ" (5:23).

Today's Gospel calls for the use of one of the texts set to Nicolai and
Bach's Wachet Auf. Nicolai's text appears variously as " 'Sleepers,
Wake!' A Voice Astounds Us," "Wake, Awake, for Night Is
Flying," and "Wake, O Wake! With Tidings Thrilling." In smaller
congregations this may be best managed by the choir.

The following hymn by Laurentius Laurentii (tune, Lancashire)
melds together the day's Gospel and the recent observance of All
Saints Day.

> Rejoice, rejoice, believers,
> And let your lights appear;
> The evening is advancing,
> And darker night is near:
> The bridegroom is arising,
> And soon he draweth nigh.
> Up, pray, and watch, and wrestle:
> At midnight comes the cry.
>
> The watchers on the mountain
> proclaim the bridegroom near;
> go forth as he approaches
> with alleluias clear.
> The marriage feast is waiting;
> the gates wide open stand.
> Arise, O heirs of glory;
> the bridegroom is at hand.

The saints, who here in patience
their cross and suff'rings bore,
shall live and reign for ever
when sorrow is no more.
Around the throne of glory
the Lamb they shall behold;
in triumph cast before him
their diadems of gold.

Our hope and expectation,
O Jesus, now appear;
arise, O Sun so longed for,
o'er this benightred sphere.
With hearts and hands uplifted,
we plead, O Lord, to see
the day of earth's redemption
that sets your people free.

The references to a bridal feast suggest the celebration of the Eucharist on this day, since the bridal setting establishes one of the great eucharistic images in the New Testament.

Proper Twenty-eight
Sunday Between November 13 and 19 Inclusive

Old Testament Texts

Judges 4:1-7 are the opening verses of the story of Deborah the prophetess and judge. Psalm 123 is a cry to God for help.

The Lesson: *Judges 4:1-7*

Faith in a Topsy-Turvy World

Setting. The book of Judges consists of a series of short stories that follow a set four-part pattern in which (1) Israel sins, (2) God judges or punishes Israel by having a neighboring nation threaten them, (3) Israel cries for help out of their situation of need, and (4) God raises up a savior in the form of a judge, who leads Israel against their enemy. The overarching sin of Israel, which takes somewhat different forms in distinct contexts throughout the book, is that they did not defeat all the nations of Canaan as God had commanded them (Judges 1:22–2:5). This situation is summarized in the divine speech in 2:3 where God states, "So now I say, I will not drive them [the Canaanite nations] out before you; but they shall become adversaries to you, and their gods shall be a snare to you." Because Israel was not pure in their quest of holy war and, instead, made treaty alliances with different nations for the sake of security, God turns these nations into an ongoing threat for Israel. Thus the book of Judges has a certain paradoxical twist in that what Israel thought it was doing for security,

143

in fact, becomes a source of continuing insecurity. The parade of judges who march across the pages of this book represent God's answer to Israel's cry for need when a neighboring nation becomes their enemy. The story of Deborah in Judges 4–5 is the third such episode in the book (see the first two stories of Othniel and Ehud in Judges 2).

Structure. The story of Deborah occurs in two forms. There is a narrative account in Judges 4 and a poetic account in Judges 5. An examination of the differences between the two accounts far exceeds the limited scope of the present study. The contrast does underscore how the lectionary text is from the narrative account. But the boundaries of the lectionary text present a problem because Judges 4:1-7 includes little more than the introduction to the story of Deborah.

Judges 4 separates into two parts. Verses 1-11 provide an introduction by describing the Canaanite threat and by introducing all of the important characters to the story: King Jabin of Canaan (v. 2), his commander Sisera (v. 2), the prophetess and judge Deborah (vv. 4-5), the commander Barak (v. 6), and the Kenites (v. 11) who are important because Jael, the wife of the Kenite Heber, is going to kill Sisera. Vv. 12-24 are an account of the battle that takes place between the Canaanites and the Israelites/Kenites. Judges 4 can be outlined in the following manner.

I. The Setting and the Introduction of Characters (vv. 1-11)
  A. Israel's Sin (vv. 1-3)
    1. Israel sins (v. 1)
    2. God judges/threatens Israel through King Jabin of Canaan and Sisera (v. 2)
    3. Israel cries to God for help (v. 3)
  B. God's Response
    1. Deborah summons Barak for holy war (vv. 4-7)
    2. Barak's equivocation (v. 8-10)
    3. The Kenites camp at Kedesh (v. 11)

II. The Battle (vv. 12-24)
  A. Barak defeats Sisera's army (vv. 12-16)
  B. Jael, the Kenite, kills Sisera (vv. 17-22)
  C. Summary statement of God's victory over King Jabin (vv. 23-24)

Significance. What is the significance of Deborah in this story? How is she a hero of faith? These questions cannot be answered if the lectionary text is limited to vv. 1-7, because the heroic quality of her character is defined in relation to the other characters in the chapter, especially Barak. Thus the lectionary reading should include at least the exchange between Deborah and Barak in vv. 8-9.

Deborah and Barak represent two very different faith stances at a moment of crisis. Deborah is being idealized as a prophet and judge who trusts in God at all costs. She delivers a message of holy war to Barak in vv. 6-7, and again, in the moment of confrontation with the superior Canaanite army, she is the one who is able to see God marching before Israel and thus is able to lead the army of Barak in battle (v. 14). Barak is a more calculating person in this story. Even though he is presented as a holy warrior with no less than ten thousand troops, when he is confronted by the prophetic summons of Deborah, he hesitates. He then responds in v. 8 with a condition. He will go into battle only if Deborah accompanies him.

The story does not condemn Barak, but neither does it idealize him. He is average. Instead, the point of focus is on Deborah and later on Jael, who kills Sisera with a tent peg. They are heroes. And given Deborah's comment to Barak in v. 9, the heroic role of women in this holy war is meant to be a surprising reversal of what was expected. That the mighty warrior Barak, with his ten thousand troops could be upstaged by two women, even though he actually fights the holy war, makes this a topsy-turvy story of faith. The reason why Deborah and Jael are stronger than Barak, and thus idealized instead of him, is that they did not hesitate in participating in God's holy war. They neither calculated the cost to their personal safety nor weighed carefully the social implications of driving a tent peg through a man's head while he

145

was sleeping, even though the bedouin rule of hospitality was most likely the highest ethical norm in this culture. They simply acted. The preacher of this text may wish to reflect on where his or her congregration is merely average in faith, where it hesitates before acting, and where it is heroic.

The Response: *Psalm 123*

A Communal Complaint

Setting. There is some debate in the commentaries concerning how Psalm 123 should be classified. Is the psalm a complaint or is it a psalm that expresses communal confidence in God? Upon first glance a debate concerning whether the psalm is an expression of confidence or complaint seems so extreme, almost like comparing oranges and apples. Yet both elements are strong in Psalm 123, which raises the question of how they relate.

Structure. The following structure of Psalm 123 will follow the set pattern of a communal complaint, which includes three parts: confession of trust, petition, and description of the present situation.

    I. Confession of Trust (vv. 1-2)
       A. God dwells in heaven (v. 1)
       B. God is merciful (v. 2)
   II. Petition for Mercy (vv. 3*a*)
 III. Description of the Present Situation (vv. 3*b*-4)

Significance. The structure of the communal complaint illustrates how the very act of petitioning and complaining to God implies a high level of trust in God. The psalmist begins Psalm 123 by anchoring two non-negotiable realities about God—namely, that God sits enthroned in heaven and that God embodies the quality of mercy. The first confession is a statement about absolute power (God is all-powerful, God is in heaven), and the second confession provides content to this power during times of suffering (the all-powerful God is merciful). Once the reality of God is confidently confessed, then the content of

God's power in a situation of suffering can be requested and even demanded (Have mercy on us, O Lord). The concluding section of the psalm describes the present experience of the psalmist in order to provide evidence to God that, indeed, the situation merits divine mercy.

The summary of the psalm illustrates how the whole structure of the complaint is built on an unwavering faith in the power of God to act. This insight provides a point of contact with Judges 4. Each text idealizes faith as something that must be sure in believers so that we act without hesitation. Judges 4 and Psalm 123 explore this kind of faith in two very different contexts. Judges 4 is a story about faith that takes charge no matter what the cost (Deborah, Jael), while Psalm 123 is about faith that is unwavering in its expectation for God to act (communal complaint psalm). The first text is about action (fighting a holy war), while the second is about passivity (calling on God to act). Yet both are about the same faith. When the two texts are read together they illustrate how both the participation in Holy War and in communal lament are heroic acts of faith.

New Testament Texts

Both lessons are concerned with "the day of the Lord." They explicate in different ways the meaning of the day of final judgment for the living of daily life as a Christian. Both lessons attempt to encourage an active, responsible, productive life of faith.

The Epistle: *I Thessalonians 5:1-11*

The Day of the Lord Directs Us in Daily Living

Setting. After instructing the Thessalonians about the destiny of those believers who die prior to the coming of Christ, by telling them of the events associated with Christ's coming (see last week's epistle), the apostles give further teaching concerning other eschatological matters in the verses of this Sunday's lesson. The subjects shift now

147

from the coming to the day of the Lord and the believers' proper concern with that day.

Structure. Commentators find an unfolding argument in these verses: First, the apostles focus on "the day of the Lord" (vv. 1-3); second, they turn to the Thessalonians and call for sober vigilance (vv. 4-8*a*); third, the apostles reflect upon the purpose of Christian life (verses 8*b*-10); and fourth, they direct the Thessalonian congregation to continue supporting one another and growing together. In a sense, this passage shows the apostles thinking their way backwards from "the end," through the future, and to the present.

Significance. The Thessalonians were apparently well-schooled concerning the promised day of judgment. The use of the phrase from the Old Testament, "the day of the Lord," suggests that scripture was studied in thinking about the coming of Christ. Perhaps we should follow the apostles' lead here and engage the text with our congregations for educational purposes. Too often we have surrendered these strange texts to social groups that operate in secretive sects on the fringes of Christianity or to support groups that use the language to construct elaborate schemes for spiritual warfare. Our own lack of concern with such passages is often a point of condemnation in charges that the Church has moved away from scripture. A serious struggle with this passage may help us in more ways than one.

The clear teaching of this and other similar New Testament texts is that "the day of the Lord" will come as a complete surprise. Christians have no advantage in knowing when God's judgment will be executed by Christ in a full and final fashion, but we do have the privilege of knowing for sure that the judgment is coming. We do not know "when," but we do know "that" the day of the Lord is coming. Furthermore, we know that the Lord is none other than Jesus Christ "who died for us, so that whether we are awake or asleep we may live with him" (v. 10). Therefore, judgment should not dismay us, for we live with the assurance that God is a God of grace.

With this knowledge and assurance we recognize the difference that our faith in Jesus Christ makes in our lives. Our identities are given through the work of God in Christ. We are "children of the light and children of the day"—that is, we live our lives before God and in conformity with God's will. Living for God means that we live vigilantly. Thus the apostles employ military metaphors to describe our existence. Notice that the hardware mentioned is purely protective, implying that God has provided for our security in life, which frees us to live according to the famous Pauline triad—in faith, love, and hope. (The parallel passage in Ephesians 5:10-17 is more expansive and includes a sword of the Lord, the Word of God, which is also wielded defensively). The association of faith and love with the breastplate and of hope with the helmet is striking. Faith is for now and hope is for the future, but love is associated with the present, and we know from other passages in Paul's epistles (especially I Corinthians 13) that love has no end.

In this passage the apostles treat every aspect of Christian life. Remarkably no part of our existence—present, future, or eternal—is left untouched by the saving work of Christ. The outcome of the assurance of salvation is a security that sets us free to live our lives for others. We do not simply "rest assured"; rather, we "act assuredly" by providing others with the kind of encouragement that ensures the mutual growth of the members of the body of believers. Once again eschatology motivates ethics. The Christians' concern with the future is not stargazing; it is the substance of a forward-looking active life.

The Gospel: *Matthew 25:14-30*

Entering the Joy of the Master or Landing in Outer Darkness

Setting. The lesson is Matthew's version of a parable that he shares with Luke, which is found in Luke 19:11-27. Scholars conclude from comparing the stories that Matthew moved this parable into the setting of Jesus' eschatological discourse as part of the expansion of that material in Matthew's Gospel. Since Matthew frames the material in an eschatological manner, it is crucial to read the text in the context of final things. Together the theme of the master coming and going and the mention of his coming to settle the accounts "after a long time" make it clear that the parable is an allegory for the second coming of Christ.

Structure. The parable opens in v. 14 with a reference that connects this story to the idea of "the day" in v. 13 and the preceding section. Verse 14 also starts the first scene of the parable (vv. 14-15), which tells of the master entrusting his property to the slaves and then leaving. With that situation established, the story continues in vv. 16-18 by reporting the slaves' uses and the non-use of the grants from the master. The parable pivots on v. 19 with the return of the master, who sets about the work of settling accounts. The business of reckoning comprises vv. 20-30, but in this final scene we should notice the extended statement by the master that forms a small speech which basically condemns the unproductive slave (vv. 26-30). Also worth notice is the aphorism in v. 29, which is set in the larger speech but which probably once had an independent existence and may even be isolated for reflection today.

Significance. As Matthew shapes and locates this text in the context of Jesus' teaching about the day of judgment, which is the time of the coming of Christ, he communicates a straightforward message to the members of his own church: Christ has departed and is going to return, and though the time seems long, we have been given a commission and we are to be about the faithful execution of Christ's charge to us. This basic message has nuance! We are not to be paralyzed by our fears, so that we actually do nothing. At the coming of Christ, fear will be no excuse for failure to follow through on Christ's directions.

At its heart this message is far more than a pep-talk, and Matthew's Jesus is doing more than issuing a threat. Notice how the story begins. The master hands out his property. The sums given are remarkable, although we miss this fact because the parable reports the amount in "talents." A talent was approximately 12,000 days wages, or the earnings of over thirty-eight years of full-time labor; so even the slave with but one talent held an extraordinary sum in trust. While it is the case that Christ was raised and we are waiting for his coming, already we have been given extraordinary riches of grace. We cannot live pitiful little lives of fear with the excuse that we are helpless, for already our Lord has endowed us with enormous grace. And as Christ entrusts us with what is his, he commissions us to pursue the responsible use, the multiplication, of his grace. Grace employed abounds, but grace buried does nothing.

Inherent in this parable is a message of grace, and coupled with the recognition of the gifts that God has given us is the promise of judgment. The parable ends with the startling threat of condemnation, but it begins with the entrusting of property and proceeds on a joyous note through the settling of accounts with the first two servants. The parable is threat, but as such it strives to motivate lethargic recipients of grace into the productive life of faith that finally hears the master say, "Well done, good and trustworthy slave; you have been trustworthy in a few things, I will put you in charge of many things; enter into the joy of your master."

Sermons that only threaten are often ineffective, merely turning off the hearers. But in fact, the majority of elements in this parable are positive—though the master's lengthy speech overwhelms us with the recognition of possible condemnation. While no sermon on this text should lose sight of the fate of the one-talent slave, major attention should be given to the trust given us, the charge to use the trust, and the promise of reckoning with the good news of the call "into the joy of [our] master."

Proper Twenty-eight: The Celebration

The Gospel lesson suggests the use of Thomas Ken's great hymn, "Awake, My Soul, and With the Sun," as the opening hymn today. The following stanza, generally omitted from North American hymnals, is the point of reference to the Gospel images. It should be printed in the bulletin to be included between the first and second stanzas.

> Redeem thy misspent moments past,
> And live this day as if thy last;
> Improve thy talent with due care;
> For the great day thyself prepare.

Also in relation to the Gospel, Wesley's hymn "A Charge to Keep I Have" is appropriate as a sermon hymn. His hymn "Talk with Us, Lord, Thyself Reveal" serves well today as an introduction to the Prayers of the People. Since even the United Methodists have removed this text from their hymnal, it is reprinted here. The tune Gräfenburg or another more meditative common meter tune may be used.

> Talk with us, Lord, thyself reveal,
> While here o'er earth we rove;
> Speak to our hearts, and let us feel
> The kindling of thy love.
>
> With thee conversing, we forget
> All time and toil and care;
> Labor is rest and pain is sweet,
> If thou, my God, art here.
>
> Here, then, my God, vouchsafe to stay,
> And bid my heart rejoice;
> My bounding heart shall own thy sway,
> And echo to thy voice.
>
> Thou callest me to seek thy face,
> 'Tis all I wish to seek;
> To hear the whispers of thy grace,
> And hear thee inly speak.
>
> Let this my ev'ry hour employ,
> Till I thy glory see;
> Enter into my Master's joy,
> And find my heaven in thee.

During the coming week, the birthday of Sojourner Truth on November 18, 1797, will be observed. Her story can be illustrative of the use of what appeared to be a minimal talent and what she was able to do with what she had.

The epistle offers the intriguing option of presenting Christ the Thief. This is not one of the standard images of Christ, not one we ordinarily think of, but it occurs more than once in the New Testament. Read Paul Minear on the subject of Christ as thief.

The New Testament writers . . . did not hesitate to speak of Christ as a robber, for they recognized that the Messiah takes from men the treasure in which they have trusted, and he does this before they are aware of their loss. . . . One may suspect that the early tradition was not without motive in selecting two other "thieves" to share the agony of Calvary with the Christ. . . . So insidious was Jesus' attack upon earthly treasures that he became, according to Kierkegaard, a "far more terrible robber" than those who assault travelers along a highway. Jesus assaulted the whole human race at the point where that race is most sensitive: its desire for security and superiority. (Paul Minear, *Christian Hope and the Second Coming* [Philadelphia: Westminster, 1954], pp. 132-33)

The benediction mentioned for last week would also be appropriate for today.

Proper Twenty-nine (Christ the King) Sunday Between November 20 and 26 Inclusive

Old Testament Texts

Ezekiel 34:11-16, 20-24 is a description of God as a good shepherd. Psalm 100 is a song of praise.

The Lesson: *Ezekiel 34:11-16, 20-24*

God as the Good Shepherd

Setting. There are two central images in Ezekiel 34, shepherds and sheep. The image of a shepherd is used in this chapter to refer to kings and the power of monarchs to lead the people of Israel, their sheep. The imagery of this chapter, therefore, relates well to the Reign of Christ Sunday.

Structure. An overview of Ezekiel 34 is necessary for interpreting the specific verses of the lectionary. The larger text can be outlined in the following manner.

I. Judgment Against Past Shepherds (vv. 1-10)
   A. Indictment (vv. 1-6)
   B. Verdict (vv. 7-10)
II. God as Shepherd (vv. 11-24)
   A. Divine search and care for the scattered sheep (vv. 11-15)

  B. Divine judgment of the sheep (vv. 16-23)
    1. The problem with the sheep (vv. 16-19)
    2. The divine response (vv. 20-23)
      a. Divine judgment (vv. 20-22)
      b. A Davidic shepherd (vv. 23-24)
III. Cosmic Implications of God's Shepherding (vv. 25-31)

The chapter begins in vv. 1-10 with judgment oracles against past kingly shepherds for not feeding the sheep, strengthening the weak, or curing the sick. The result of their harsh use of power is that the sheep roam the mountains without direction. Most sheep farmers would agree that this is not a particularly healthy situation for sheep. The situation leads to judgment oracles against the past shepherds, which, we are told in v. 10, is how God will save the sheep from the shepherds. Verses 11-24 describe how God will take the place of the past shepherds, and vv. 25-31 show what implications God's action will have on all nature.

The lectionary text is made up of verses from the middle section of the chapter. Verses 11-15 describe how God will search out and care for the sheep. Verse 16 provides a transition from the image of God seaching for lost sheep (vv. 11-15) to the image of God judging between different kinds of sheep (vv. 17-22, the lectionary text has omitted vv. 17-19, which state a problem of power that exists between different sheep). Verses 23-24 end this section by describing how God will establish once again a Davidic shepherd.

Significance. Christ the King Sunday is a celebration of the kingship of Jesus, or to state it another way, it is a celebration of Jesus' sovereignty. This is a Sunday that celebrates power from a hierarchical perspective. The king is not just any leader in ancient Israel. The king is in a special position of power and authority. Given this background, what does it mean to celebrate the power of Christ as king?

The central metaphor for describing the power of kings in Ezekiel 34 is shepherd. The image reinforces our earlier conclusion about hierarchy because it immediately prompts a distinction with sheep.

Yet the image also begins to provide content to what the power of sovereignty means. Heirarchical structures of power in the Old Testament frequently function as an inversion. Thus to have power over others means that it must be used in favor of those with the least power. The king, therefore, in ancient Israel (and throughout the ancient Near East) was judged by how well he cared for the widow or the orphan. This criteria is the basis for God's judgment of past kings in Ezekiel 34:1-10, and it is also the basis for judgment between the sheep in vv. 20-22.

In summary, Ezekiel 34 says at least five things about hierarchical power, which can be explored in preaching, depending on what issue may relate to your congregation. First, that hierarchies of power are inevitable (vv. 1-10). Second, that such structures of power are easily abused by humans in a number of ways (vv. 1-10, 17-22). Third, that a proper understanding of such power is not innate to us, but actually requires that God become the shepherd in order to show us how it works (vv. 17-22). Fourth, once God has shown us what the character of royal power is, we can claim this Davidic ideal in the present time (vv. 23-24). And, fifth, that the realization of this ideal has cosmic implications (vv. 25-31). Ezekiel provides powerful tools both for interpreting Christ the King and for reflecting on what discipleship means because Christ now rules.

The Response: *Psalm 100*

A Hymn of Praise

Setting. Psalm 100 evokes images of the cult. There is a call to worship in v. 2 along with encouragement to enter the sanctuary. These images reappear again in v. 4 with more precision, when the worshipers are instructed to pass through the gates of the Temple and then to enter into God's court.

Structure. The hymn divides into two sections. Verses 1-3 are an extended call to worship culminating in the recognition formula that all worshipers must "know that the LORD is God." Verses 4-5 intensify the call to worship with the imagery of a procession into the Temple.

Significance. The central image of the psalm for worship on Christ the King Sunday is the royal imagery of God as being the shepherd of the people of God in v. 3. This is framed within the larger setting of a recognition formula, which suggests that in worship the people of God must come to realize that they are sheep in God's pasture. The recognition of God as being the shepherd of the worshiping community leads to three conclusions about the character of God in v. 5. God is a good shepherd, God embodies covenantal love (steadfast love), and God's love is unending. This revelation is the basis for praise in the psalm.

New Testament Texts

The text from Ephesians is a grand expression of thanksgiving that recognizes and celebrates God's saving power in Jesus Christ. The lesson from Matthew is the well-known final judgment scene, where the power of God is applied by Christ in separating the sheep and the goats.

The Epistle: *Ephesians 1:15-23*

Thanking God for the Riches We Have in Christ

Setting. We first encountered Ephesians during Year A as the epistle lesson for the second Sunday after Christmas day when Ephesians 1:3-6, 15-18 was the reading. The following discussion repeats parts of that earlier discussion.

Normally Pauline letters open with a greeting, as Ephesians does in 1:1-2, and then follows a prayerful thanksgiving prior to the beginning of the body of the letter. Ephesians, however, has a blessing of God for the blessings Christians have received (similar to a Jewish *berakah*) in 1:3-14; and then, 1:15-23 is the usual thanksgiving prayer report.

Structure. There are two broad, related movements in the lesson.

First, in vv. 15-19, hearing of the believers' faith in the Lord Jesus and of their love of the saints, Ephesians

   I. Gives Thanks for the Believers
  II. Asks That God May Give the Believers a Spirit of Wisdom and Revelation Resulting in the Knowledge of God
     A. For their illumination unto hope (part of God's call),
     B. For an awareness of their inheritance among the saints,
     C. For an appreciation of God's great saving power.

Then, Ephesians shifts the focus in vv. 20-23 to comment on God's mighty working in Jesus Christ. Thus, the meditation (and possibly the preacher's sermon) takes a christological turn, both remembering and declaring

  III. God's Resurrection of Christ,
  IV. God's Exaltation of Christ Over
     A. All powers and places,
     B. All names in all times, and
   V. God's Making Christ the Head of His Body, the Church, Which Now Shares the Benefits of His Glory.

Significance. These lines from the thanksgiving of the letter (1:15-18) unpack the meaning of God's blessings for us as believers and members of the Church. The prayer asks that God give to the believers the gift of intimate comprehension of God. Such understanding is not knowledge that comes through human ingenuity or effort—such as knowledge which comes from studying a textbook. Rather, Ephesians asks for the gift of God's self-disclosure, which would come as an ever-deepening relationship between God and the believers. This kind of knowledge is charismatic and mysterious and comes as God works in our lives, not as we grasp after unseen things. In relation to God, the life of believers is characterized by the joy of hope and an awareness of the richness of God's grace. Believers have a new attitude, but it is not the result of positive thinking; it comes purely as a gift from God, and it activates a new way of living. Verse 19 makes this clear by speaking of "the immeasurable greatness of his power for us" and of "the working of his great power."

With this mention of God's magnificent power, the thanksgiving takes a christological turn to illustrate the clearest testimony to God's power—namely, the Resurrection of Christ. As is normal in New Testament thought, Ephesians refers to the Resurrection as something that God did. Though Christology articulates and illustrates the truths of God, God never takes the back seat to Jesus Christ. This manner of thinking is the pattern of early Christian reflection, and from time to time we have to remind ourselves that the glory of divine radiance emanates from God, lest we lose sight by blocking God out with a "Son umbrella." As we meditate on Christ, we ponder the greatness of God.

The passage continues by recalling the range of Christian conviction in relation to Christ, speaking of his exaltation, his power over all other powers, and his relationship to the Church, which participates in his majesty. As the first mention of God's power in v. 19 stated that it was/is "for us," so now in v. 22 we read that God "has put all things under [Christ's] feet and has made him the head over all things for the church." In this christological mediation that ultimately celebrates the powerful work of God, there is a deep conviction that what God has been about in Christ has profound significance for the Church. This idea often causes discomfort for Christian theologians living and working in comfortable settings, for the passage seems "triumphalistic" or "self-aggrandizing." But we have always to recall that these lines were most likely composed when Christians did not have any worldly power and, in fact, were facing opposition and persecution. Far from celebrating current power and status, these lines are a critical statement of faith about God's grace and generosity that would sustain believers in difficult circumstances. We should avoid using these lines to excuse our tendency toward living in luxury.

The Gospel: *Matthew 25:31-46*

The Final Judgment of the Nations

Setting. The prophecy of the final judgment of the nations comes as the final section of Jesus' eschatological discourse in Matthew 24-25. The description of the end is a fitting ending for this part of the Gospel, for all that went before in the discourse pointed forward to this very scene. Immediately after this teaching Matthew moves us into the story of Jesus' suffering, death, and Resurrection.

Structure. The story presents a clear and uninterrupted account that develops logically. "The Son of Man" appears in power. Then, he separates the individuals from all the nations, "The sheep from the goats." In turn, he addresses each group, first the sheep and then the goats. After each address by "the king," the members of the groups respond. When they have spoken in chorus, the king pronounces his verdict. For shaping a sermon in relation to the form of the text, it is crucial to notice the content of the sections as well as their order. The ideas inherent in the passage that should be treated in proclamation are (1) Christ is coming for judgment, (2) judgment means separation, (3) the standards for the division are striking, (4) both the sheep and the goats are surprised, and (5) Christ has the last word.

Significance. The news that Christ is coming to judge the nations should take no one in a Christian congregation by surprise. The New Testament states this conviction over and over, but what to make of the message? The most basic way to apply this message to our lives is to take seriously that God is active; God has standards, so that not everything goes; and God promises to reckon reality and human existence in relation to God's standards. Jesus Christ is to act as judge, and we know something about who he is, how he lived, and what we can expect him to do in God's behalf. As God's standards were revealed by Christ, they will be applied by Christ.

The idea of separation, goats from sheep, is difficult; but it is a striking part of the biblical vision and message. Again, not everything goes with God. Many of our actions and many of our attitudes have no place in God's kingdom, and through the separating judgment of Christ, God effects a separation that purifies, that winnows, that establishes the right and eliminates the wrong. Remarkably, in Matthew's Gospel the notion of such separation is always held for the future. The present is a mixture of the kinds, but the promise of separation should startle us to examine our own ways before Christ does.

In this story we find a remarkable standard for the separation. Christ judges the peoples of all the nations in terms of whether they did or whether they didn't give food to the hungry, drink to the thirsty, hospitality to the stranger, clothing to the naked, care to the sick, and comfort to those in prison. We read nothing in Christ's list about a profession of faith, and indeed the last thing the sheep seem to have had was a personal relationship with Jesus Christ. This is not a slam at contemporary evangelical concerns, but it is a reminder that purely personal piety is not all that Christ calls for and expects. This scene of a final judgment is part of Matthew's total Gospel, and in that complete work there are other passages that balance this one with its heavy emphasis on action. Moreover, Matthew's Gospel finds its place in the context of the canon of scripture from which it is clear that a strong relationship between God and the human(s) is indeed a central part of God's purposes of working through the history of Israel and in the person of Jesus Christ. The heart of the gospel is that we have a relationship to God in Christ and we find the directions for our living, both by grace.

One of the curious elements of this story is that both the sheep and the goats are surprised. The sheep have served Christ without knowing him, and the goats have known Christ without serving him. The surprise in this final judgment is that Christ does not deal with those who both know and serve him. The lesson tells us about the fate of all but active Christians, so that we are given a pair of lessons: First, we learn of Christ's capacity to judge those who have never known him. Second, we are shown that lip service is not enough. More than anything this text strives to startle complacent Christians into an active life of faith.

Finally, despite the surprise and the protests of both groups, Christ's judgment stands. Excuses don't work. Thus clearly the authority for judgment rests with God, not with us.

Proper Twenty-nine: The Celebration

Today brings us to the end of the Christian year with its ringing affirmation of the reign of Christ who "fills all in all" (Ephesians 1:23). Through the lessons we see that Christ's rule is analogous to the caring shepherd (Old Testament), that it is universal (epistle), and that Christ's judgment of the world is based upon loving action rather than doctrinaire attitudes (Gospel).

Perhaps more badly conceived sermons with works righteousness as their aim have been preached on Matthew 25:31-46 than any other text in holy scripture. So many guilt trips have been laid upon people and so much homiletical righteous indignation vented because of the numbers of the hungry unfed, the naked still unclothed, the imprisoned unvisited. Given how frequently that text has been employed in the twentieth century, particularly as the primary canon of the social gospel, it is surprising to find the social conditions worse in the United States than in the rest of the less "religious" countries of the industrialized West. The difficulty is that preachers have used the text to talk about how the Church should be dealing with the world, when in fact it has to do with how the world should be treating the Church! And its Gospel surprise is that God graciously judges those who deal lovingly with God's people whether they "name the name of Christ" or not. This is a characteristic of Matthew's proclamation, as we may recall from the story of the two brothers sent to work in the field. Today's parable distinguishes between "the nations" and "the least of these." For Matthew "the least of these" are the followers of Christ, and "the nations" are the powers of this world. Too often Christian preachers have assumed a kind of triumphalistic stance in relation to this parable, portraying the Church as the agency (usually backed by plentiful U.S. funding) entrusted with cleaning up all the world's ills, an ecclesiastical version of the white man's burden. We have tried to use Matthew to preach Luke. Matthew, however, suggests that our attitude towards the world is to be that of ''the least,'' not United Way. This is not to say that the Church has no concern for the social ills enumerated in the parable, but for this parable that is not the point. The point is that because Christ rules, a lot of people will experience salvation not because of what they say but because of what they do. Having Christ in charge can be a very disturbing business, but never dull.

This is a christological feast, meaning that hymn texts that use the words *Lord* and *King* need to be examined closely to be certain that the point of reference is the Second Person of the Trinity. ''Come, Thou Almighty King'' or ''O Worship the King'' refer to the First Person of the Trinity, and so do not reinforce the day's theme. Not all worship resources or topical indexes in hymnals seem to appreciate the distinction, so worship planners should take care. Two of the scriptural images can be combined by using the metrical version of the psalm, ''The King of Love My Shepherd Is.''

Thanksgiving Day

Old Testament Texts

Deuteronomy 8:7-18 is a sermon by Moses calling Israel to remember that their good life in the land is a gift from God. Psalm 65 is a hymn.

The Lesson: *Deuteronomy 8:7-18*

Giving Thanks

Setting. Deuteronomy 8 is part of a larger section of literature that includes chapters 6–8, in which Moses exhorts Israel to keep the law. This section looks at law from a number of different perspectives. Law is introduced with the promise of blessing in 6:1-3, and it is equated with love in 6:4-9 ("Love the LORD your God with all your heart."). Then law is examined in relationship to God's gift of the land in 6:10–8:20. Even though Israel's present life in the land is the prominent setting for these chapters, the perspective changes somewhat between 6:10–7:26 and 8:1-20. Deuteronomy 6:1–7:26 underscores how Israel's gift of the land was not a result of any inherent characteristics of theirs, but the result of God fulfilling past promises, and that faithfulness to God requires that they risk everything to following God into the land no matter how powerful the surrounding nations may appear. The point of this section is that such risk will lead to blessing.

Deuteronomy 8:1-20 shifts the focus to explore how Israel can continue to be faithful to God even after they receive divine blessing and hence are no longer in a threatening situation in the land. Thus there is a progression in this section from initial problems of Israel being threatened in the land by other occupants (6:10–7:26) to a very different kind of problem—namely, the threat of security, when their own power to produce food and to guard the land seems to be sufficient (8:1-20). The first section (6:10–7:26) is focused exclusively on the promise of land in its call for Israel to risk everything in following God. Once the land is secured, the second section (8:1-20) goes back in time and focuses on the wilderness in order to remind Israel that their real source of security lies someplace else rather than in the power of their own resources to produce a good life. The setting of the text suggests that the people of God must be constantly aware of the wilderness in order to be able to give thanks to God in the land. The following interpretation will explore this point in more detail.

Structure. The lectionary has incorporated aspects of Deuteronomy 8:1-20. It has eliminated the opening exhortation for Israel "to remember" the wilderness and how God provided for all of their needs as they traveled through it. This experience of complete dependency in the wilderness is described as Israel's theological education by God: It was in the wilderness that God disciplined Israel (v. 6). Verses 7-18 (19-20) begin another cycle of preaching by Moses, which separates into three parts. Verses 7-10 set the stage for the sermon by describing Israel's future life in the land as one of bounty. Verses 11-18 are an exhortation for Israel not to forget God during such times of bounty. Verses 19-20 describe the consequences of forgetting. The middle two sections (7-10 and 11-18) constitute the boundaries of the lectionary text.

Significance. Deuteronomy 8 is a challenging and helpful text for worship on Thanksgiving Day, for it cautions us about the dangers of giving thanks. Note how the text presupposes that the people of God are indeed thankful. Verse 10 reads: "You shall eat your fill and bless the Lord your God for the good land that he has given you." Thus the danger of this text is not that Israel will lack piety and proper forms of ritual, once they are secure and prosperous in the land. The danger is much more subtle and sinister, it is whether they will actually be giving thanks to God or themselves by saying, "My power and the might of my own hand have gotten me this wealth" (v. 17).

The problem of giving thanks to God during times of prosperity is not the rituals, but whether we can see God behind them. Security is often accompanied by religious blindness, with the result that thanksgiving can become a complex form of self-gratification. Moses addresses this problem in Deuteronomy 8 by locating Israel's self-identity outside of the land altogether, back in the wilderness. Note how the text is dominated by the positive command "to remember" and the negative command "not to forget." These two commands complement each other by underscoring to Israel how their self-identity cannot begin with the situation of bounty in the land. The reason for this shift back in time (from Israel's present situation in the land to their past travel in the wilderness) is to remind Israel that power (and security) is not what it seems, especially at those times when it appears to be so clear during times of bounty. This insight that the wilderness is the starting point for identity rather than the land makes thanksgiving to God possible.

Deuteronomy 8 addresses the problem of security in giving thanks to God. Thus the text addresses a common problem for congregations in the North American context, but it certainly does not address all congregations. If your congregation finds itself in a threatening situation at this time of thanksgiving, then Deuteronomy 8 is not an appropriate text. The preacher may wish to shift the focus from Deuteronomy 8:1-20 to Deuteronomy 6:10–7:26 which is a call to faithfulness at a time of risk.

The Response: *Psalm 65*

A Hymn

Setting. Psalm 65 fits well as a response to Deuteronomy 8 for it picks up elements of thanksgiving. Some scholars have even suggested that the psalm was meant to function as thanksgiving song of the harvest feast in ancient Israel. Others, however, have suggested that the psalm originally consisted of two separate hymns, a more communal thanksgiving in vv. 1-8 and a more individual hymn in vv. 9-13.

Structure. Whether or not Psalm 65 was an original unity, it lends itself to such a reading in its present form by suggesting a separation into three sections (vv. 1-4, 5-8, 9-13). Verses 1-4 introduce praise of God in Zion. Verses 5-8 celebrate the power of God as creator from a more universal perspective. Finally, vv. 9-13 narrow the focus from praise of God's cosmic power to praise of God's ability to deliver rain and to provide bounty.

Significance. Psalm 65 complements Deuteronomy 8 by providing language of praise that points the worshiper beyond his or her own power to provide. In so doing, Psalm 65 provides the proper language for thanksgiving. The logic of the psalm anchors the worshiping community firmly in the sanctuary as the place where God's bounty is to be discerned (vv. 1-4). Once the setting of worship has been established, the subject matter of praise ranges from God's cosmological power as creator of the world (vv. 6-8) to God's more immediate power as of the created order (vv. 9-13).

New Testament Texts

The readings bring together remarkably different texts—an epistolary appeal and a Gospel miracle story—from remarkably different contexts: Paul's work in assembling a collection for the poor Christians in Jerusalem and Jesus' peripatetic ministry. Although the epistle reading treats the topic of generous giving and the Gospel lesson teaches about the nature of true worship, they are brought together because of their mutual concern with "thanksgiving." One minister noticing these readings for Thanksgiving Day said, "Well, there you have it; that's what Thanksgiving's about: praising God and taking up the collection!" At one level the meanings of both passages are self-evident, but the readings also have in common a subtle complexity related to profound theological themes.

The Epistle: *II Corinthians 9:6-15*

The Gracious Gift of Generosity

Setting. Sometime after Paul wrote I Corinthians, a group of outsiders arrived in Corinth. These people were Christian preachers, but their message was that Christianity was a vitally renewed Judaism wherein certain people possess the power to work miracles. These preachers claimed to possess that extraordinary power, indeed they maintained they were sources of divine power. Paul referred to these people as "super-apostles," a clearly sarcastic designation in the apostle's use, but a title which may have been their self-designation. Although the super-apostles clearly came from Jewish-Christian circles, they were like other Hellenistic religious propagandists of that day who had a flashy, obviously powerful style of ministry—powerful in proclamation and powerful in deeds.

There are distinguishable sections to II Corinthians. The recognizable portions of the letter are so distinct that many scholars conclude the canonical letter is a later editor's compilation of preserved passages (fragments?) from more than one earlier letter. Whether or not this is the case, II Corinthians 8–9 are devoted to comments and directions concerning the collection Paul assembled among his predominantly Gentile-Christian churches for the impoverished Jewish-Christian congregation in Jerusalem.

Structure. The text has two broad movements of thought that are intricately related to each other. In vv. 6-10 Paul explicates the idea that God gives the ability to be generous; in turn, vv. 11-15 explain that when believers are generous, their generosity glorifies God. The obvious themes for proclamation are the divine origin of generosity, the divine character of generosity, the gracious experience of generosity—as giver and recipient—and the thanksgiving that results from generosity which glorifies God.

Significance. Paul admonishes the Corinthian Christians to generosity. The reason: You reap what you sow. How often this text and similar others have been abused! But Paul does not say that

Christians give to get or that giving assures receiving more. Paul's talk about "seed" faith operates on a higher level than the merely mundane. Paul says elsewhere that he had learned to live in all circumstances, from plenty to want. He never says he has a secret to ensure prosperity. What we see in this passage is that the generosity practiced by Christians is not equated with niceness, but with godliness. God gives freely so that we can be like God—free and cheerful givers.

The central issue in Paul's reflection is righteousness. We see this clearly in the quotation of the Septuagintal version of Psalm 111:9 (English = Psalm 112:9) and in the commentary on the scripture citation in v. 10. God's fundamental character is righteousness—that is, God's faithfulness in redeeming sinful humanity. Our generous God supplies for us what we as humans cannot provide—namely, forgiveness and a new, eternal relationship to God through our Lord Jesus Christ.

In seeing this focus of Paul's thought, we should not be surprised by the direction he takes in vv. 11-15. The generosity to which Paul calls the Corinthians and for which God blesses them is a demonstration of faith and love, so that those who receive the provisions from the Corinthians offer thanks to God. Those who give and those who receive are united in mutual devotion to God—despite their very real human differences. The Corinthians are predominantly Gentiles and relatively well-off, but the Christians in Jerusalem are ethnic Jews who have fallen on very hard times. The distinctions are racial, cultural, and economic; yet Paul understands that God's graciousness recognizes no such boundaries. God's generosity crosses the sin-set structures of human relations in clear demonstration of the power and authority of the gospel of Christ.

Note well that Paul does not call the Corinthians to give to increase their fortune and fame, rather they give for the glory of God. Thus in concluding his remarks about generous giving, Paul breaks forth into doxological expression which literally says, "Grace to God for his indescribable gift!" In context, we see Paul identifying a theological "what goes around comes around." Verse 14 speaks of the "grace of

God" and v. 15 declares "grace to God"; so that we see God as the source and uniting goal of all grace.

The Gospel: *Luke 17:11-19*

The Wholeness of Faith

Setting. In chapter 3 Luke tells of the appearance of the adult Jesus in the context of the ministry of John the Baptist. After narrating certain preliminary events (for example, the temptations of Jesus) Luke begins in chapter 4 to tell about the ministry of Jesus in Galilee. At Luke 9:51, however, we learn that Jesus turned dramatically toward Jerusalem; then, from Luke 9:51–19:27 Jesus is on the road to Jerusalem. All along the way he says and does remarkable, memorable things that constantly defy normal expectations. The lesson tells of Jesus' encountering and healing ten lepers during the journey to Jerusalem.

Structure. At a glance the account is a miracle story, but the events reported alter the normal pattern of an ancient miracle story. Usually a miracle is recounted by telling of the problem, the action of the healer in relation to the difficulty, and the confirmation of the miracle. Here, however, Jesus' action, a command to the lepers to go and show themselves to the priests, takes the lepers off the scene so that we do not get the usual immediate and dramatic confirmation. Rather, Luke as narrator tells us they were cleansed after their departure, and then we read about the return of the thankful Samaritan. Both Jesus' action and the subsequent events are noteworthy, and in the following comments we will examine some of the details. For now, we may recognize that the story sequence itself is suggestive for the pattern of homiletical reflection: the lepers' cry for help, Jesus' command to do the law, the obedience of the lepers, the return of the Samaritan giving thanks, Jesus' strange complaint about the mere obedience of the other lepers, and Jesus' enigmatic closing declaration.

Significance. The ten lepers had a problem, and as we learn from this story the problem was so great that normal social and religious boundaries were set aside as nine (?) Jews and a Samaritan were united in their misery. All were ostracized from normal society; all were feared and even despised by others, so that the old hostility and sharp distinctions between Jew and Samaritan were irrelevant.

To the leper's credit they turned to Jesus for help. Somehow they heard and believed that he could resolve their difficulty. The lepers stood at a distance so as not to run the danger of rendering Jesus and his companions actually and ritually unclean through contact with them. There was not much science in the medical diagnosis or handling of "leprosy" in the first century, so to understand this text we need to see how the lepers were regarded and how they regarded themselves, not to collect facts about Hansen's disease and psoriasis. The recognition of Jesus' authority is inherent in their address, "Master!"

In response to the cry of the lepers, Jesus, who had the authority and power to heal them, issued a command. He told them to do exactly what was required by the law, to show themselves to the priests who would confirm their health. The problem and its solution are framed as religious issues, not merely medical matters. The ancient recognition that God is the ultimate source of all true healing is too often lost in a world that turns to pills more often than to God. (More on this point later!)

As the lepers went, Luke tells us they were cured and that one of them, noticing his condition, returned to Jesus. The language of vv. 15-16 in Greek is the technical vocabulary of worship, specifically of doxology, prayer, and thanksgiving. The former leper praises God and humbles himself in thanks before Jesus. Here we see a clear recognition of the power of God at work in the ministry of Jesus. The report of the man's actions is an implicit christological statement about the person of Jesus. Yet, as the following verses show, the Christology is vitally related to the reality of life.

Luke records that the man was a Samaritan. Perhaps in the context of the early Church's struggles with Judaism this point was preserved for polemical purposes. Nevertheless, the distance between where the story was first told and read and the context in which we encounter the story today is so great that all possibility of using this account as a critique of Judaism is gone. Rather, what is to be critiqued today is the tendency merely to do what is necessary to get what we need for life without ever bothering to stop and give rightful thanks to God for all life's blessings. If we have a headache and taking aspirin works the cure, why thank God? Because the substance, the science, and the scientists that made the aspirin are parts of God's creation; they are even God's gifts to humankind.

When we see God as the power and source of all good, we become like the one leper, not like the nine. And, as in faith we praise God in thankfulness, we indeed stand with the Samaritan in hearing the word of Jesus' blessing. Faith that perceives God and thanks God qualitatively alters the condition of our lives, for through it we have a relationship to God that makes us whole. Literally translated, Jesus says, "Your faith has made you whole." This point is easily misunderstood, but notice that Jesus did not say, "Because you have faith you have been made well." Christian faith itself is always to be understood as God's gift to us which enables the relationship to which God calls us in Jesus Christ. Faith itself is perhaps the gift for which we should, especially on Thanksgiving Day, give thanks to God.

Thanksgiving Day: The Celebration

The challenge to preacher and to worship planners on this day is to maintain a proper balance between the purely national or patriotic character of the day and the independence of the pulpit to proclaim to the nation both the judgment and the grace of God. We are to avoid being reduced to civil chaplains on the one hand, but we also need to avoid that kind of self-righteousness which maintains that if the church isn't doing it, God isn't in it.

The Old Testament lesson will remind us of how America has identified with the story of Israel. A re-reading of William Bradford's *Of Plymouth Plantation 1620–1647* can be a good annual exercise for preachers at this time of year. The catch to identifying with Israel is that the identification must go all the way—not only with the chosenness, but also with the rebellion, with the refusal to acknowledge that chosenness may be for inclusivity rather than exclusivity.

The epistle reminds us of our obligations to others as a response to God's gifts to us. The eucharistic offertory can be used as an illustration here. The practice of the primitive Church, a society that dealt in kind rather than cash, was for members to bring bread and wine to the offertory. Enough was set aside for the Lord's Supper, but the remainder was sent to the ill and the poor who could not afford food. Hence, every meeting at the Lord's Table was a time of sharing God's gifts with others. This is the basis for the special offering for the poor that is observed by many churches at communion time. An offering of money or goods may also be received at this service, whether eucharistic or not.

The Gospel lesson brings home the importance of gratitude as an element of Christian life and faith. The Christian's response to God's loving action is a eucharistic one.

The traditional thanksgiving hymn, "Come, Ye Thankful People, Come," is particularly appropriate at this time of year, because it connects with the advent themes which will have been a part of the recent Sunday readings and which will be continued on the First Sunday of Advent. Some suggested hymns related to the texts are:

Old Testament: "All People That on Earth Do Dwell"
"God of Our Fathers [the Ages], Whose Almighty Hand"
"Stand Up and Bless the Lord"
"O Worship the King, All Glorious Above"
"We Gather Together to Ask the Lord's Blessing"
Epistle: "God, Whose Giving Knows No Ending"
"Lord, Speak to Me That I May Speak"
"Take My Life, and Let It Be"
"We Give Thee But Thine Own"
"What Does the Lord Require"
Gospel: "God, Whose Love Is Reigning O'er Us"
"Let All Things Now Living"

"Let Us with a Gladsome Mind"
"O What Shall I Render"
"When All Thy Mercies, O My God"

White is the color for this thanksgiving service, and the church may be decorated with symbols of the harvest. If the Eucharist is celebrated, the Table should not be turned into a worship center with a cornucopia that displaces the primary gifts of bread and wine. To have the bread and wine produced by members of the congregation would be particularly fitting on this day.

Scripture Index

Old Testament

A Comparison of Major Lectionaries

YEAR A: TIME AFTER PENTECOST (PROPERS 18–29, ALL SAINTS DAY, AND THANKSGIVING DAY)

	Old Testament	Psalm	Epistle	Gospel
PROPER 18 (September 4-10)				
	[RoCath: 23rd Ordinary Time]		[Luth: 17th After Pentecost]	
RCL	Exod. 12:1-14	149	Rom. 13:8-14	Matt. 18:15-20
RoCath	Ezek. 33:7-9	95:1-2, 6-9	Rom. 13:8-10	
Episcopal	Ezek. 33:(1-6) 7-11	119:33-48	Rom. 12:9-21	
Lutheran	Ezek. 33:7-9	119:33-40	Rom. 13:1-10	
PROPER 19 (September 11-17)				
	[RoCath: 24th Ordinary Time]		[Luth: 17th After Pentecost]	
RCL	Exod. 14:19-31	114 or Exod. 15:1b-11, 20-21	Rom. 14:1-12	Matt. 18:21-35
RoCath	Sir. 27:30–28:7	103:1-4, 9-12	Rom. 14:7-9	
Episcopal	Sir. 27:30–28:7	103	Rom. 14:5-12	
Lutheran	Gen. 50:15-21	103:1-13	Rom. 14:5-9	

	Old Testament	Psalm	Epistle	Gospel

PROPER 20 (September 18-24)
[RoCath: 25th Ordinary Time]

[Luth: 18th After Pentecost]

	Old Testament	Psalm	Epistle	Gospel
RCL	Exod. 16:2-15	105:1-6, 37-45	Phil. 1:21-30	Matt. 20:1-16
RoCath	Isa. 55:6-9	145:2-3, 8-9, 17-18	Phil. 1:20-24, 27	
Episcopal	Jonah 3:10–4:11	145	Phil. 1:21-27	
Lutheran	Isa. 55:6-9	27:1-13	Phil. 1:1-5 (6-11), 19-27	

PROPER 21 (September 25–October 1)
[RoCath: 26th Ordinary Time]

[Luth: 19th After Pentecost]

	Old Testament	Psalm	Epistle	Gospel
RCL	Exod. 17:1-7	78:1-4, 12-16	Phil. 2:1-13	Matt. 21:23-32
RoCath	Ezek. 18:25-28	125:4-9	Phil. 2:2-11	Matt. 21:28-32
Episcopal	Ezek. 18:1-4, 25-32	25:1-14		Matt. 21:28-32
Lutheran	Ezek. 18:1-4, 25-32	25:1-9	Phil. 2:1-5 (6-11)	Matt. 21:28-32

	Old Testament	Psalm	Epistle	Gospel
	PROPER 22 (October 2-8)			
	[RoCath: 27th Ordinary Time]			
	[Luth: 20th After Pentecost]			
RCL	Exod. 20:1-4, 7-9, 12-20	19	Phil. 3:4b-14	Matt. 21:33-43
RoCath	Isa. 5:1-7	80	Phil. 4:6-9	Matt. 21:33-43
Episcopal	Isa. 5:1-7	80	Phil. 3:14-21	Matt. 21:33-43
Lutheran	Isa. 5:1-7	80:7-14	Phil. 3:12-21	Matt. 21:33-43
	PROPER 23 (October 9-15)			
	[RoCath: 28th Ordinary Time]			
	[Luth: 21st After Pentecost]			
RCL	Exod. 32:1-14	106:1-6, 19-23, 47	Phil. 4:1-9	Matt. 22:1-14
RoCath	Isa. 25:6-10	23	Phil. 4:12-14, 19-20	
Episcopal	Isa. 25:1-9	23	Phil. 4:4-13	
Lutheran	Isa. 25:6-9	23	Phil. 4:4-13	

	Old Testament	Psalm	Epistle	Gospel
		PROPER 24 (October 16-22)		
		[RoCath: 29th Ordinary Time]		
		[Luth: 22nd After Pentecost]		
RCL	Exod. 33:12-23	99	I Thess. 1:1-10	Matt. 22:15-22
RoCath	Isa. 45:1, 4-6	96:1-5, 7-10	I Thess. 1:1-5	Matt. 22:15-21
Episcopal	Isa. 45:1-7	96		
Lutheran	Isa. 45:1-7	96	I Thess. 1:1-5a	Matt. 22:15-21
		PROPER 25 (October 23-29)		
		[RoCath: 30th Ordinary Time]		
		[Luth: 23rd After Pentecost]		
RCL	Deut. 34:1-12	90:1-6, 13-17	I Thess. 2:1-8	Matt. 22:34-46
RoCath	Exod. 22:20-26	18	I Thess. 1:5-10	Matt. 22:34-40
Episcopal	Exod. 22:21-27	1		
Lutheran	Lev. 19:1-2, 15-18	1	I Thess. 1:5b-10	

	Old Testament	Psalm	Epistle	Gospel
PROPER 26 (October 30–November 5)				
[RoCath: 31st Ordinary Time] [Luth: 24th After Pentecost]				
RCL	Joshua 3:7-17	107:1-7, 33-37	I Thess. 2:9-13	Matt. 23:1-12
RoCath	Mal. 1:14–2:2, 8-10	131:1-3	I Thess. 2:7-9, 13	
Episcopal	Micah 3:5-12	43	I Thess. 2:9-13, 17-20	
Lutheran	Amos 5:18-24	63:1-8	I Thess. 4:13-18	Matt. 25:1-13
PROPER 27 (November 6-12)				
[RoCath: 32nd Ordinary Time] [Luth: 25th After Pentecost]				
RCL	Joshua 24:1-3a, 14-25	78:1-7	I Thess. 4:13-18	Matt. 25:1-13
RoCath	Wisdom 6:12-16	63:2-8	I Thess. 4:13-17	
Episcopal	Amos 5:18-24	70		
Lutheran	Hosea 11:1-4, 8-9	90:12-17	I Thess. 5:1-11	Matt. 25:14-30

	Old Testament	Psalm	Epistle	Gospel
PROPER 28 (November 13-19)				
[RoCath: 33rd Ordinary Time]				
[Luth: 26th After Pentecost]				
RCL	Judges 4:1-7	123	I Thess. 5:1-11	Matt. 25:14-30
RoCath	Prov. 31:10-13, 19-20, 30-31	128:1-5	I Thess. 5:1-6	
Episcopal	Zeph. 1:7, 12-18	90	I Thess. 5:1-10	Matt. 25:14-15, 19-29
Lutheran	Mal. 2:1-2, 4-10	131	I Thess. 2:8-13	Matt. 23:1-12
CHRIST THE KING OR REIGN OF CHRIST SUNDAY				
PROPER 29 (November 20-26)				
[RoCath: 34th Ordinary Time]				
[Luth: Last After Pentecost]				
RCL	Ezek. 34:11-16, 20-24	100	Eph. 1:15-23	Matt. 25:31-46
RoCath	Ezek. 34:11-12, 15-17		I Cor. 15:20-26, 28	
Episcopal	Ezek. 34:11-17	95:1-7	I Cor. 15:20-28	
Lutheran	Ezek. 34:11-16, 23-24	95:1-7a	I Cor. 15:20-28	

ALL SAINTS DAY

	Old Testament	Psalm	Epistle	Gospel
RCL	Rev. 7:9-17	34:1-10, 22	I John 3:1-3	Matt. 5:1-12
RoCath	Rev. 7:2-4, 9-14	24:1-6		
Episcopal	Sir. 44:1-10, 13-14	149	Rev. 7:2-4, 9-17	
Lutheran	Isa. 26:1-4, 8-9 12-13, 19-21	34:1-10	Rev. 21:9-11, 22-27 (22:1-5)	

THANKSGIVING DAY

	Old Testament	Psalm	Epistle	Gospel
RCL	Deut. 8:7-18	65	II Cor. 9:6-15	Luke 17:11-19
RoCath	I Kings 8:55-61	113:1-8 or 138:1-5	Col. 3:12-17 or I Tim. 6:6-11, 17-19	or Mark 5:18-20
Episcopal	Deut. 8:1-3, 6-10 (17-20)		James 1:17-18, 21-27	Matt. 6:25-33
Lutheran	Deut. 8:1-10		Phil. 4:6-20 or I Tim. 2:1-4	

A Liturgical Calendar

September Through Christ the King 1993–2001

	1993 A	1994 B	1995 C	1996 A	1997 B
Proper 17	Aug. 29	Aug. 28	Sept. 3	Sept. 1	Aug. 31
Proper 18	Sept. 5	Sept. 4	Sept. 10	Sept. 8	Sept. 7
Proper 19	Sept. 12	Sept. 11	Sept. 17	Sept. 15	Sept. 14
Proper 20	Sept. 19	Sept. 18	Sept. 24	Sept. 22	Sept. 21
Proper 21	Sept. 26	Sept. 25	Oct. 1	Sept. 29	Sept. 28
Proper 22	Oct. 3	Oct. 2	Oct. 8	Oct. 6	Oct. 5
Proper 23	Oct. 10	Oct. 9	Oct. 15	Oct. 13	Oct. 12
Proper 24	Oct. 17	Oct. 16	Oct. 22	Oct. 20	Oct. 19
Proper 25	Oct. 24	Oct. 23	Oct. 29	Oct. 27	Oct. 26
Proper 26	Oct. 31	Oct. 30	Nov. 5	Nov. 3	Nov. 2
Proper 27	Nov. 7	Nov. 6	Nov. 12	Nov. 10	Nov. 9
Proper 28	Nov. 14	Nov. 13	Nov. 19	Nov. 17	Nov. 16
Proper 29 (Christ the King)	Nov. 21	Nov. 20	Nov. 26	Nov. 24	Nov. 23

	1998	1999	2000	2001
	C	A	B	C
Proper 17	Aug. 30	Aug. 29	Sept. 3	Sept. 2
Proper 18	Sept. 6	Sept. 5	Sept. 10	Sept. 9
Proper 19	Sept. 13	Sept. 12	Sept. 17	Sept. 16
Proper 20	Sept. 20	Sept. 19	Sept. 24	Sept. 23
Proper 21	Sept. 27	Sept. 26	Oct. 1	Sept. 30
Proper 22	Oct. 4	Oct. 3	Oct. 8	Oct. 7
Proper 23	Oct. 11	Oct. 10	Oct. 15	Oct. 14
Proper 24	Oct. 18	Oct. 17	Oct. 22	Oct. 21
Proper 25	Oct. 25	Oct. 24	Oct. 29	Oct. 28
Proper 26	Nov. 1	Oct. 31	Nov. 5	Nov. 4
Proper 27	Nov. 8	Nov. 7	Nov. 12	Nov. 11
Proper 28	Nov. 15	Nov. 14	Nov. 19	Nov. 18
Proper 29 (Christ the King)	Nov. 22	Nov. 21	Nov. 26	Nov. 25